TAKING AWAY THE KEYS

A Momoir

LANE MORRIS BUCKMAN

Copyright © 2021, 2022 The Outside

Lane Books All rights reserved.

No part of this book may be reproduced in any form or by any electronic or mechanical means, including information storage and retrieval systems, without written permission from the author, except for the use of brief quotations in a book review.

Cover art by aaftabi

Ebook ISBN: 9780990647379

Print ISBN: 9780990647324

For all the caregivers who would rather be doing anything else.

Introduction

For as long as I can remember, the car was my mother's happy place. I sometimes feel like I was born on wheels. Given that our first home was a single-wide trailer set back in the woods of Jack- sonville, North Carolina, where my dad was stationed at Camp LeJeune, maybe I was.

Lonely, after my father was deployed to Vietnam before I was two months old, and far from her family home at Fort Benning, Georgia, my mother would wrap me in blankets, put me in the passenger seat of her MGB, and drive for comfort. When I cried at night, she would drive me around until I fell asleep. Finally, she drove me all the way to Fort Benning, where we stayed until my father came home and we moved into another trailer in Buford, South Carolina.

I have vague memories of that time. Although, one that is tattooed in my memory is how my baby teeth marks looked when I bit into the patterned vinyl seats of the Ford LTD my parents were driving. I did a lot of biting in that car. My mother did a lot of cruis-ing. Sometimes she would drive straight through 400 miles from South Carolina to Georgia to have coffee with my grandparents at

Introduction

the Sambo's on Victory Drive, before turning around and driving right back home.

When we moved to Aurora, Colorado, I nearly killed myself a couple of times in that car. I liked to play with the big silver door handles, and I have another very clear memory of how it felt when the door swung open wide, and I started falling toward the pave- ment that whooshed by, only to be pulled back inside the car by my hair. Car seat laws and child safety locks were put in place because of toddlers like me.

While I can't recall driving to Georgia from Colorado, we did put a lot of miles on the light blue, four-door on the road between Aurora and Colorado Springs, where my mother's brother was stationed. Then, my father was transferred to Japan, and we moved back home, where we drove between sets of grandparents in Phenix City, Alabama and Fort Benning a few times a week.

Mom would take me for long rides out on the reservation at Fort Benning, or up to Pine Mountain, Lookout Mountain, or Stone Mountain–we did a lot of winding roads up steep inclines in another MGB.

My mom was a terrible driver even then. She was a speeddemon and didn't pay a whole lot of attention to what was going on around her. She was usually singing at the top of her lungs, or tryingto play with me. Twice, she had accidents in that car where I ended up in the emergency room, once having slammed the radio out ofthe dashboard with my head. I had knob-shaped indentations in my forehead for a week.

When my dad came home from Japan, we moved to Norfolk, Virginia and the forty-eight-hour turnaround trips to Georgia resumed. Mom would put me in the car when she got off work, and she would drive like something was chasing her until we met my grandmother at the Krystal. Sometimes we'd go back to their house and Mom would take a nap, but then we were right back on the road.

A little over a year after we moved, my father was transferred up to D.C. We stayed behind in Norfolk so I could remain in my

Introduction

school. Mom was driving another in a string of MGBs that my father would buy on the cheap and restore to re-sell.

This one had a big hole in the passenger seat floorboard and you had to be careful not to drop anything while you were driving, or it was gone. Including your feet. After that was an Austin Healey that Mom had to hotwire to start. The horn was attached to a doorbell that hung down from the dashboard, and the soft-top was rusted open. Mom would make a nest of blankets in the floorboard, put me in it with a cup of hot chocolate (I had to work not to spill), wrap more blankets around me and drive me to school while it snowed into the car.

She made it fun.

By the time we moved to Texas, we'd been through so many cars I couldn't name them. There were at least six more before we got to the silver Thunderbird we bought after my mother fell asleep at the wheel on one of her frantic drives to Georgia. She drove off the highway in Meridian, Mississippi and we flew over the edge of a ravine. The car flipped three times and landed in a copse of trees, where we sat dazed until Good Samaritan onlookers came to our rescue.

Our move to Texas coincided with, and was rooted in the collapse of her marriage, so the car became my mother's safe space. She and my dad fought all the time and she didn't want to go home. So, she would pick me up from school and on nights we didn't go straight to the mall and shop until closing time, she would drive aimlessly through the Dallas/Fort Worth metroplex until dark. And then had the audacity to ask me why I hadn't done my homework.

Throughout my childhood, I can guarantee you that aside from the hours I was in school, I was in a car more than I was outside of one. By the time I could drive, I had been in at least two accidents per year with my mom, and watched her accept more speeding tickets than I could tell you about.

My mother loved to drive.

In the year leading up to me grounding her, her driving had become even worse. She was running red lights without even blinking, ignoring stop signs if she didn't see other cars waiting, losing

Introduction

her way on roads she'd traveled for years, and had terrified at least two of her friends enough that they had called me and asked if I could do something about her. When I took her keys, she cried. Then she screamed. Then she begged.

She cycled through all the stages of grief save for acceptance for two years. I'm not sure she's hit acceptance yet, honestly. She still fantasizes about what she's going to do when she escapes her memory care home, reminding me that she knows how to jimmie a lock and hotwire a car. "I don't even need keys," she tells me with a knowing smile.

So, I consider myself fortunate that the symptoms of Vascular Dementia and fallout of a stroke mean that while she can fantasize and plan, she can't put those two things together long enough to do more than threaten me with her two-wheel-drive terrors.

This is our story. It is a story about a mother and a daughter, dementia, and dealing with it. This is my momoir about taking away her keys.

More than just her keys, it's what those keys symbolize: my mom's freedom. In taking ownership of my mother's keys, I have locked myself into a journey with her as her caregiver. We are both passengers in a car driven by dementia, each of us equally helpless and sometimes hopeless, but just like she always did for me, I'm going to do my level best to make it fun.

I May Not Have Seen It All, But I've Seen Plenty

The People and Problems I've Cared For

This is a book about caring for a loved one (LO) with dementia. Specifically, it's the story of me caring for my mother and her transition from sound mind and body, to "Oh dear…we have a problem." I'm not a doctor, or a therapist, or a scientist, or any kind of technical expert.

What I am is an individual with thirty-five plus years of continual and increasingly responsible experiences with various types of dementia and the people who have had it.

I have helped care for Loved Ones with diagnosed Alzheimer's, with stroke-related loss of executive function and memory loss, with Sundown Syndrome, and with vascular dementia. I've cared for LOs who have lost language skills, who were legally blind, who were trapped in their beds by sickness, and who were escape artists. I have cared for Loved Ones in their homes with my own hands, with the assistance of sitters, with the assistance of full time helpers, and in nursing homes, and in senior communities.

I have fed my adult Loved Ones, changed their diapers, bathed them, dressed them, cleaned their teeth for them, ferried them to and from appointments they never would have kept for themselves, learned to manage medical equipment and clean feeding tubes and catheters, and dress wounds, and all sorts of things I never imagined I would be doing.

I have dried their tears of pain, confusion, frustration, anger, helplessness, and hopelessness.

I have held their hands while they died, or met the ambulance at the hospital when it was too late to save them crying my own tears of frustration and helplessness, or trying to shove all those emotions deep inside to deal with later. I am the queen of the five-minute meltdown, where I set a timer and give myself a few minutes to be hysterical before pulling it together to go again.

I write this book from the perspective of someone who has been there in the trenches--who is still in the trenches. I write as someone who has an endless supply of empathy for you as a Caregiver (CG).

My hope is that when you read this book, you feel seen and validated, and that maybe when you put it down for the last time, you walk away from it with some helpful tips, feeling (at the very least) okay about how you are doing in your own journey.

This book is a hybrid of how-to and personal experience, peppered through with conversations I've had with my mom since dementia took over our relationship. I'm going to get very personal with you about my experience, especially my experience with my mom. I hope you'll hang in there with me through the truth that I hate being a caregiver, and I hate that I hate being a caregiver because on the other side of how I feel is what I do to overcome the feelings. At the end of the day, I think I'm a better person for facing my fears and doing what is right, some days only because I know Karma is watching.

A Momversation

Ring Ring
    Me: Hello?
    Mom: [crying] Hi! How are you?!
    Me: Okay—what's wrong, Mom? Why are you crying?
    Mom: Oh, Lane. I'm stuck in a time warp.
    Me: What do you mean?
    Mom: Well, I'm ashamed to tell you. I went out to a club with my friends and they were all drinking. They asked me if I wanted a drink. I knew I shouldn't, but I said yes. Lane, I don't know what they put in my drink, but they drugged me and they brought me here and now they won't take me home.
    Me: That sounds really scary. Can you look around and tell me where you are? What do you see?
    Mom: I'm in a bedroom decorated just like mine. It looks just like mine with all of my things.
    Me: Then you are home. You are in [room number] at the [community name] and you're right where you are supposed to be.
    Mom: No. It's a clone. I'm in a clone room.
    But, five minutes later, I had her convinced she was okay.
    And all I can think is, *"Hey, nurse from yesterday? This is the woman*

you chose to give you business, career, and life advice?" And also, *"Why does my mother think she lives in the Matrix?"*

What is Dementia?

My mom's GP gave her the initial diagnosis of vascular dementia, and had been treating the root causes (untreated heart disease and diabetes) to help prevent further damage to her brain when she ended up in the hospital with a stroke. A psychiatrist came in to exam her (she was behaving very badly), and we spoke.

"Who told you she has dementia?" he asked me.

"Her doctor," I said.

"Why?"

"Why what?"

"Why did he say she had dementia?"

I started listing out all of the reasons and he raised his voice at me, "How did he come to the diagnosis of vascular dementia?!"

"I don't know," I said. "It was a combination of things?"

"Did he do an MRI?"

"No."

"Do you have any brain scans?"

"Just the ones they did when she came into the ER."

"And did he see those?"

"I don't know…"

"Then he can't know if she has dementia! She doesn't have

dementia! There's nothing wrong with her brain." And then he stormed out of the room.

I was stunned, and for a moment, I was frozen. All these thoughts ran through my head, chiefly a horrifying worry that I had just made up all my mom's strange behavior and was Munchausen's by Proxying her, where I was making up diseases for my mom in order to get attention for myself. All the stress and concern about whether I was doing the right things for her converged. Had I given her doctors the wrong impression of her? Was *I* crazy? Had I taken away her car keys and all her freedom for nothing? Was I abusing my mom?

But then my feet started moving and I chased him out into the hallway.

"Excuse me," I called after him. I was fighting through tears at that point, and trying to ignore the two nurses at the station desk who had looked up. "I am not a doctor. I have a degree in English Literature, so I'm not an expert in how dementia gets diagnosed, but my mom can't function on her own. She can't remember how the stove works. If you stand her in the middle of the hallway, she can't remember which way to turn to get to the dining room. She got lost in a closet last month. He didn't diagnose her from an MRI, but we got one when she had the stroke, and we also got a few different CT scans and the ER doctor said she definitely had visible damage. There is absolutely something wrong with her brain."

He stared at me for a moment then said, "Well, I need to see her in my office anyway. Schedule an appointment."

I did not say, "Like hell." I just went back to my mom's room. A little while later, a nurse came in with a knowing smile. "Some of them think they are gods," she said. "When you talk to the social worker, did you know they have a list of all the available doctors in your area? By which insurance they take?"

I did not know that, but was glad to hear it. And that was how we found my mom's psychiatrist.

The Stages of Dementia: Alzheimer's and General Dementia

Once you have a diagnosis, you might start wondering, "Where are we in this journey?" If you're me, you wonder more bluntly, "How long is this going to last?"

Dementia as a diagnosis is fairly nebulous and can mean a lot of things. It isn't specific. It's an umbrella term for a grab bag of awful symptoms, like "Karen" is an umbrella term for a grab bag of bad behaviors. Alzheimer's is an actual diagnosis of a very specific disease with very specific stages, that follows a general path of destruction. Because it is a specific disease, some treatment may be available and more, and more progress is being made on that front every year.

With a degenerative disease like Alzheimer's you might hear about three stages, Early, Middle and Late with progressions characterized by levels of independence or ability to care for oneself. In the Early Stage, a person might be able to live independently and help make decisions for their future, but they start to find it increasingly difficult to do things they've always managed to do easily before. Forgetfulness and an inability to retain new information can be part of this stage.

In the Middle Stage, a person needs help with the day-to-day.

You might see big personality changes in this stage. This is the stage in which people might start getting lost, forgetting where they live, or how to dial the phone. They might start to experience incontinence. Hopefully, they might be able to participate in hobbies and interests, and might be able to be on their own for short amounts of time, but they definitely need to be in a safe environment.

Late-stage Alzheimer's is characterized by a need for round-the-clock care. In the Late stage, a person isn't really able to initiate engagement or activity. It might be hard for them to communicate. It might even be difficult for them to communicate pain or discomfort. This is the stage in which comfort becomes key.

With other types of dementia, you might hear about seven stages. WebMD characterizes these stages below:[1]

1. No impairment. Someone at this stage will show no symptoms, but tests may reveal a problem.
2. Very mild decline. You may notice slight changes in behavior, but your loved one will still be independent.
3. Mild decline. You'll notice more changes in their thinking and reasoning. They may have trouble making plans, and they may repeat themselves a lot. They may also have a hard time remembering recent events.
4. Moderate decline. They'll have more problems with making plans and remembering recent events. They may have a hard time with traveling and handling money.
5. Moderately severe decline. They may not remember their phone number or their grandchildren's names. They may be confused about the time of day or day of the week. At this point, they'll need assistance with some basic day-to-day functions, such as picking out clothes to wear.
6. Severe decline. They'll begin to forget the name of their spouse. They'll need help going to the restroom and eating. You may also see changes in their personality and emotions.
7. Very severe decline. They can no longer speak their

thoughts. They can't walk and will spend most of their time in bed.

I would say that my mom was in Stage 2 for several years before she made a crashing fall into Stage 3. From Stage 3 into Stage 4 was less than a year.

I moved my mom into an independent living community in October 2017. By December, a home health care nurse had told me that I needed to prepare myself for a swift and serious decline. "These disorders happen in levels," she said. "But it's not like goingdown a hill. It's like falling off a cliff. One day they can do their laundry. The next day, they just can't. It's going to happen, and it's going to happen fast."

My mom teetered between Stages 4 and 5 for several months before landing firmly on her backside (literally, she started falling down a lot) with a marked decrease in executive function.

Stages 2 and 3 for my mom just looked like annoying, erratic behavior. It looked like someone who was just getting old and crotchety, and forgetful. Stage 4 looked like forgetting how to use a smart phone, then a flip phone in a matter of weeks. She went from calling all the time to not calling at all because she couldn't work her phone anymore. She got lost in her own closet a few times, as in, she opened the door, looked inside the closet and couldn't remember how to turn around, so she panicked that she had been kidnapped. (Fortunately, she had a flip phone then, and could still dial it. I talked her through turning around and getting out of the closet.)

Stage 5 looks like an inability to learn any new names. She knows who she knows and if she didn't meet you before 1990, she isn't ever going to meet you—she will just introduce herself to you on an endless loop. She doesn't get lost in her closet anymorebecause it has ceased to exist for her. She knows closets exist, she knows she has a closet, but when she looks at the closet doors she's just not making the connection between what she is seeing and the concept behind it.

For us, for her, Stage 5 looks a lot like how I feel when I realize I've zoned out of a conversation and missed a whole chunk of information, or when I'm driving and realize I have zoned out and have no idea how I've already gotten to work because I barely remember getting on the highway. Sometimes, it looks the way I feel when I have searched all over the house for the car keys, only to find them in plain sight. My mom is just zoned out. She connects where she can, and she's confused, afraid, angry where she cannot.

Stage 5 has really frightened me, to tell the truth. Stage 5 makes me cry a lot more than Stage 4 did. It was a lot easier to find the humor in Stage 4. In Stage 4 it was pretty easy to distill my mom's disease into charming, entertaining anecdotes. I find it more and more difficult to do that now because Stage 5 is also extremely annoying.

Since Mom can't remember that she's already asked me how my dogs are, she asks me multiple times in a visit. How are the doggies? How are your puppies? How are the dogs? Each time, it's a brand new question to her. Each time, it's a reminder to me that there is less and less of her. A friend of mine likened his father's dementia to a dry erase board that had his entire life written out from left to right, starting with his birth, running through the day dementia robbed him of his first memory. "And it was like someone had just taken an eraser and wiped out the whole last 2/3s of the board, and some spots in the middle. They could come erase more and more every so often, until finally all that was left was his childhood, and then not even that."

My friend warned me, "But the emotions are all still there. They can't remember what the emotions are connected to, but they are still there. They still yearn, and sometimes, that's worse."

My mom was very athletic in her youth. She played baseball, she danced, she ran, she boxed, she rode her bike everywhere and roller-skated. By the time I came along, or by the time I was old enough to notice, she really didn't do much physically. She didn't even like going for walks. Stage 5 of dementia for her means her entire identity is tied up in how sporty she was as a youth. That's who she thinks she is now. She is convinced that the only thing holding her back from being an Olympic-level athlete today is me.

She is deeply upset with me because I haven't done more to help her get her brain back, and I haven't done enough to help her get back into fighting shape. What does that look like to her? More doctor appointments for sure! But, also, I need to be enrolling her incollege so she can learn how to remember, and I need to be taking her to sports therapists.

Recently, while visiting with a surgeon, I got really frustrated with her because she didn't understand exactly what was going on, only that her legs were involved, and she wanted assurances that as soon as any surgery was done, she would be able to sprint or do cross-country running again. Again. Right. I was sitting there staring at the side of her head thinking, "Woman, you haven't run more than the length of a hallway since 1985. Ain't no magic going to have you in Usain Bolt's slipstream."

The surgeon's assistant told her of course she'd be able to run because that's how you're supposed to deal with dementia. You're supposed to agree with it and hope it doesn't call your bluff in a week.

We got back in the car and Mom was thrilled that I had finally gotten her some help, and she was finally going to get to play baseball again. She started telling me all the things she was going to do as soon as she'd had her "meniscus repaired"-because she's sure that we were seeing the doctor about her "torn meniscus". She did not have, nor has she ever had a torn meniscus.

This is where I really struggle with my ego because I hate being wrong, or looking stupid, and in my mom's eyes I have been wrong, and I have trusted in my own ignorance over her vast medical knowledge. That was sarcasm, if it didn't come across. She has no medical knowledge, buts she fully believes I haven't done enough to help her get healthy so she can be active. That appointment cemented the belief for her.

She was so validated and victorious, and was just chattering about all the things she is going to do once we get her knee fixed, and I was gripping the steering wheel and gritting my teeth because

I had to concentrate on not telling her the whole truth. She wouldn't remember the whole truth, but she would remember to be upset about it, and that's worse.

I hope your Loved One grew up in a lovely household and lived a calm, peaceful life. Mine did not, so when there are gaps in her cognition, she fills those in with experience-based paranoia and danger. When she doesn't remember that she lives in a community where people do her laundry for her, she is positive those women are trying to steal her clothes.

Right now, she remembers me. She remembers I'm married to Bryan, and we have a son. She remembers her grandson, but she's always surprised to find out he isn't a toddler anymore. He's a teenager. It shocks her. Lucky for us, she's delighted with the news that my baby is now driving and getting ready to graduate high school.

She doesn't always remember that she has been divorced since 1993, or that my father remarried, or that my grandparents are dead. She doesn't always remember where she lives—scratch that. She has no idea where she lives. At a recent visit, she told me how nice it was to be vacationing at a resort in the mountains of South Carolina. She was in her memory care in the flatlands of north Texas.

My understanding is that Stage 2 for Alzheimer's and Stages 4 and 5 for other dementias are the longest periods of the disease. These periods are particularly painful for caregivers as they watch their Loved Ones slip away. It is an extremely long grief process, and honestly, a nightmarish merry-go-round of denial, anger, bargaining, depression, and acceptance until the end finally comes.

My mom and I have had a complicated relationship, but she's still my mom and I love her fiercely. When my mom's mind was whole, I really loved having conversations with her. She was funny and adventurous, and I could always count on her to listen to me. I'm not sure the advice she gave me was always great, but it came from a place of love. Now, because of her inability to process new information or strong emotion, I can't talk to her about anything beyond her community and small niceties.

I've tried to have deeper conversations with her, but they left her confused and upset, and for weeks after she would bring up snippets of my words outside of context, trying to make them fit into what she was able to remember. You know that feeling when you can't remember a word? You know that you know the word. It's on the tip of your tongue, but you just can't reach it. That's how my mom lives her life with nine out of ten thoughts. The frustration we all feel when we can't grab that word we want is the frustration my mom feels every time she tries to think about something beyond exactly what she can see.

I watch this and I see the struggle in her, and I want to hold her, and I want to fix it. I can't fix it. I feel helpless and useless, and I also feel angry and cheated. I am so angry at her disease because it has robbed me of the best of my mother. I can be sitting across the table from her while she's nattering away about something that doesn't even exist, and my insides are wailing, "I want my mom!"

I do. I want my mom. I really want my mom. All I can have is my mom's body with this weird disease in it. Dementia has hollowed her out and works her like a puppet, and I'm trapped in an inter- minable improv sketch with her, where I am just going along with whatever her disease throws at me.

I feel like a spoiled brat. I'm a grown woman throwing a fit on the inside because I'm mad at a disease. It's tempting to compare my situation to others, and tell myself to get it together because we don't have it as bad as some people do, but pain is all relative and should never be a contest, so I try to let myself have my feelings. I try to remind myself that my mother isn't the enemy, her disease is. I try to breathe through anger and fear. I try to cut myself some slack when I fail. I try to live by my motto, "Do the best you can. Then, when you learn better, do better."

While we were in COVID lockdowns, and I was sneaking up to visit her closed bedroom window while she was in strict quarantine after her roommate had been diagnosed positive, I did a pretty good job of holding myself together. The quarantine, the upset to her routine, the fear, and the loss of access to stimulation set her back quite a bit. It was really hard to watch her struggling to understand why I wouldn't come inside, or why she shouldn't open her window, or why I wouldn't take her to get a haircut or a sausage biscuit.

I tried to stay cheerful for her, but on one visit, I felt so much like Dumbo when Mrs. Jumbo is locked away from him in the jail car of the circus train, that I started sobbing at the window. I just broke down and wept like a baby. She didn't understand what was wrong, and she was putting her hand up on the window trying to get to me, and I couldn't explain it, and she couldn't hear me anyway because she had dropped her cell phone to try to comfort me. It was a mess.

I just wanted my mom. That's all. And the only thing that could have helped me was having my mom. I didn't want the confused lady at the window. I wanted my mom.

I felt so terrible for putting her in that situation. The only saving grace was that I could hope she would forget it. Happily, she did. Also, unhappily she did. It would have been nice to talk to her about it and decompress, or laugh at myself with her. Instead, the next time I visited, steeled against my own feelings, she asked me why I hadn't been to see her since she was locked away. She didn't remember me visiting at all.

A Momversation

After I had moved Mom into her first memory care community, I had a talk with the chief corporate nurse and I asked her if it was possible that seeing me was doing my mom more harm than good. Very gently she said, "It's very good that you've noticed this pattern. Many family members don't see it, or refuse to admit it. It might be best if you don't visit for a little while and let her settle in."

Because, and this was also true in the hospital for the past two months, if I skipped a day visiting, Mom did better the following day. Then, when she saw me again, she lost her mind even more.

I skipped visiting on Thursday and Friday because she had such a monster time on Wednesday. She was fine both nights. I visited Saturday morning for 1.5 hours, then by 3PM the staff was calling me, asking me to come or else they had to call the police.

She was banging on windows and busting into the rooms of other residents, terrorizing them. It took me two hours to calm her down once I got there.

So, I changed my visiting schedule and my mom was okay. She was better than okay. She started to be fine.

Meanwhile, I got this phone call while driving home from work.

. . .

Ring Ring

Me: Hello?

Mom: Lane, you have to come get me out of this place (unintelligible rambling for several seconds) and it's too much pressure, and I can't take it.

Me: What is happening?

Mom: (losing her temper) I can't live like this! I won't live like this! I will get a gun and blow my goddamned brains out! You hear me? I will blow my goddamned brains out!

Me: (making sure I breathe) I cannot come to you right now, Mom, I'm driving and I'm not near you.

Mom: Well, I'm dying! They are killing me with this pressure, Lane! I can't take it!

Me: (trying a tactic that has worked before) Mom, I need you to look around and tell me what you see.

Mom: My room.

Me: And what do you see in your room?

Mom: Lane, I'm not doing this with you right now. I'm under too much goddamned pressure and I'm going to die! I want to die! [commence animal-style sobbing]

--I pulled over so I could try to talk her off the ceiling. Ten minutes in, a nurse checked on her (she was in her room) and helped me get to the actual issue--

Long story short: The pressure was that Mom had been invited to color or paint with the other residents, and she didn't want to do either. I literally threw my hands up in the air and looked around for someone else to confirm what I was hearing. No one else in the parking lot, though.

Once a nurse and I had convinced her that she was not required to accept the invitation, and could sit in her room and read if she wanted to, she was fine.

You know that "reasons my toddler is crying" meme? I'm going to start one called "reasons my Old Person is losing it".

What Should You Know up Front

I belong to several support groups, and as I was working on the outline for this book I asked them, "If you were going to pick up a book on the caregiving experience for a Loved One with dementia, what would you want to read about or learn?" Some of their responses broke my heart.

"How do I get my family to help me?'
"I want to feel like there is hope."
"The truth. It will never get better, only worse."
"How to talk to and deal with my Loved One."

Let's break those down, though, because they are important.

Q: How do I get my family to help me?

A: If your family isn't already inclined to help you, you can't. It's sad facts. You cannot guilt, shame, cajole, or inspire people to help you with the burden if they aren't already inclined to help you. I say this from experience, from watching my friends go through the caregiving journey, and from conversations with Senior Care experts.

I have watched friends with siblings struggle to even get abrother to call and speak to a parent. One friend's older brother refused to visit because seeing his father made him too sad. It was fine for his baby sister to live with him and change her father's diapers, but just looking at his father made her brother too sad to participate in his care. And, yes, I am judging him harshly.

I have seen siblings drop a Loved One off at another sibling's door and drive off without explanation after having struggled alone as a caregiver for years. I have heard siblings say, "I can't take Mom. My marriage wouldn't survive it." I've sat across from women who were in tears because their siblings said things like, "You're better equipped to handle this," or, "You're already a stay-at-home-mom, so you're the right person to care for Dad," or, "Don't ask me again. I hated her when I lived with her, and she's not going to live with me."

The number of seniors with or without dementia, who have no one caring for, or advocating for them is shocking. One of my best friends has worked in senior social services for her entire career and I've volunteered through a few of her programs and worked to raise money or collect donations, and seen firsthand the elderly who are wasting away in facilities where they are forgotten, or struggling to survive in houses that are falling down around them, or who are languishing in hospitals with no one to be Shirley McClain from Terms of Endearment for them. Seniors aren't a sexy demographic and senior social programs are competing with homeless babies and abandoned puppies for funding and grants, so they often don't have the resources to do more within their communities.

Q: I want to feel like there is hope.

A: This really depends on what you're hoping for. If you're hoping for recovery, that's a false hope. If you're hoping for a happy ending, you have to reconcile your definition of happy with the best case scenario for death. If you're hoping that once the disease has run its course you can have a happy life, I'm right there with you!

Q: The truth. It will never get better, only worse.

A: Dementia doesn't get better. You don't go from Stage 5 back to Stage 3. You don't recover from Stage 6 back to Stage 2. It doesn't happen. The certainty of the disease is progression. What has been lost is gone, and while you may be able to delay progression, there isn't any current science that can stop it. So where does that leave hope? I don't know. I don't have any hope for my mom's recovery. What I have is the ability to give her the best care I can afford. That's all.

Q: How to talk to and deal with my Loved One.

A: This varies with the Stage in which your LO currently lives. It also varies with what you mean by "talk to" and "deal with" because a state of dementia means your LO lives in a reality that is different from yours. You cannot reason with dementia. If dementia thinks you are Diane-from-1962, then that's who you are. If dementia thinks you are your LO's mother, then that's who you are. If dementia thinks your LO is in a box car behind the Don Juan's taco stand in Grand Prairie, Texas, then that's where your LO is. Period. The best practices are to meet your LO where they are, to agree and not argue, to join them in the adventure their brain is on. Some- times that works. Sometimes it doesn't. With all respect, I find it works best for us if I treat my mother's conversation like she is a toddler, while still speaking to her like she is an adult. Toddlers don't make a whole lot of sense because they haven't mastered language and nuance. Dementia patients sometimes don't make a whole lot of sense because nuance is the first thing to go, and they can't always make connections between what they want to say and the language to say it.

A Momversation

9:17PM
   Ring Ring
   Me: Hello?
   Mom: Lane?
   Me: Yes, it's me.
   Mom: (whisper hissing like she's in a spy movie) Lane, we have a situation.
   Me: Okay, Mom. What is it?
   Mom: It's the car. You know the building where your father gets the oil changed? We're on the second floor of that building and the car is dead. I need someone to come jump us, or it's going to be dire.
   Me: I can do that for you, Mom.
   Mom: Good. Get here fast! The people are closing in on us and we don't have much time.
   Me: Mom, can you tell me where you are right now?
   Mom: I'm in the hall closet.
   Me: Well, that's not a great place to be. Can you get out of the closet?
   Mom: I guess. Why?
   Me: So you don't wrinkle your clothes. You hate wrinkled clothes.
   Mom: I do.
   Me: So, can you turn around? Tell me what you see?

Mom: *I see my bed and my chair.*
Me: *So you're in your room.*
Mom: *I am in my room.*
Me: *Great! Can you get into bed, or into your chair?*
Mom: *Oh. Well. Probably. No. I'm in the floor.*
Me: *You're in the floor?*
Mom: *Yes. I'm in the floor and I can't move because my knees are busted to bits.*
Me: *That's not good.*
Mom: *I can crawl.*
Me: *(knowing the chair is right next to the closet) The chair is very low, can you pull yourself up into it?*
Mom: *(lots of grunting) No.*
Me: *Okay, hang on.*
Mom: *Uf.*
Me: *Are you still in the floor?*
Mom: *I can't get out of the floor. I'm just rolling around here. (then, in a fake yell) Haaaalp! Haaaaalp!*
((Enlist Bryan to call the home to get help for her, while I keep her on the phone.))
((Stay on phone having weird conversations about what Mom is doing in the floor—rolling around and finding things—and how much she wants a biscuit until I hear a second voice. Mom argues with second voice, puts second voice online.))
RA: *Hello?*
Me: *Hi, I'm Joan's daughter. She called and said she was in the floor.*
RA: *Your mom isn't in the floor. She's sitting in her chair.*
Mom: **I WAS IN THE FLOOR AT ONE POINT BUT I GOT MYSELF OUT OF THE FLOOR!**
Me: *If she's out of the floor, we're good.*
RA: *Um...she wasn't ever in the floor. I was just in here to get her ready for bed.*
Me: *Okay.*
Mom: *LIAR! I WAS IN THE FLOOR!*
RA: *Here's your mom back.*
Mom: *I was in the floor.*

Taking Away the Keys

Me: I believe you. You're in the chair now.
Mom: Yes.
Me: Good.
Mom: So what do I do now?
Me: Now, it is time to go to bed.
Mom: Okay. Good. I'm tired.
Me: I bet you are. I love you.
Mom: I love you, too. Bye!
...

I have no idea if she was ever in the floor in actuality.

Uncle Abe

In 1986, I was a freshman in high school when my mother came home talking about Uncle Abe.

My mom was a banker at one of those old, independent, very posh banks in Dallas in the 80s. Uncle Abe was one of the bank customers who would come in regularly to check his accounts, ask about interest rates on CDs, and have some social time with the staff.

My mom really liked him, and enjoyed when he would come visit her at her desk. He was bright and funny, and extremely fit for his ninety years. He walked everywhere because he no longer trusted himself to drive.

At first, her stories were really funny and sweet. Then, she started to worry because he was wetting his pants when he sat in her chair. He looked like he was losing weight. He seemed frightened. Then, one day he came in and said someone had told him he couldn't live in his house anymore.

I want you to picture my mother, all five feet, two inches of her, in her 80s power suit and feathered hair, driving Uncle Abe back to his house to confront the random man who had home-invaded him, and told him the house wasn't his anymore. After he had told her the story, my mother packed Uncle Abe up into her car, took him back to his house, and went toe-to-toe with what turned out to be a grifter who was well known by the Dallas police for scamming the elderly.

The grifter put up a bit of a fight, but then ran when he heard sirens. The police who arrived on the scene were very concerned. Turned out, he was actually dangerous. It also turned out, my mother is a honey badger.

Months later, when Uncle Abe hadn't made his weekly visit, Mom went to his house and found him in a pool of his own blood. She got him to the emergency room and saved his life. He had a massively ulcerated stomach, was malnourished, dehydrated, and was having some memory problems. And that was when Uncle Abe became ours.

My mother adopted him and gained legal guardianship of him. For the next six years, Uncle Abe was our family. My mother visited him after work every day (dragging me along with her), and we spent every other weekend at his house doing chores and yard work.

Rapidly, he lost the ability to speak English, reverting entirely to his first language. Neither of us spoke Yiddish, so we were at a loss. By 1988, it was clear that Uncle Abe couldn't live alone. He wasn't able to cook for himself, or answer the landline phone, or even take care of his hygiene.

After the police called us a couple of times in the middle of the night, letting us know that Uncle Abe had been found walking down the highway, my mom found a Yiddish-speaking, Polish woman who was visiting her son on an extended Visa, and hired her to live with Uncle Abe and be his keeper. It wasn't long before she was telling us he was "crazy", and that led to some appointments with a neuropsychiatrist who gave us the diagnosis of Alzheimer's.

Now, my mom didn't believe in Alzheimer's. She believed that you could cure anything with herbs and nutrition, so she pushed aside the doctor's diagnosis and just started pumping Uncle Abe fullof ginkgo biloba and ginseng and hawthorne. There weren't any medications for Alzheimer's available back then, and my mother distrusted Big Pharma. She rejected all offers of sleep aids and mood enhancing drugs for Uncle Abe that might have made the job a little easier for his helpers.

Alzheimer's for Uncle Abe meant he thought my mother was his "Mama" and I was a random street urchin he called, "the boy." I'm not a boy. As the disease progressed, those were the only English words he used. "My mama," and "the boy."

The disease took his language skills, made his hands shake too hard to hold an eating utensil, and robbed him of every dignity, leaving him with only anger, frustration, and fear.

Ultimately, we were not able to keep helpers. Uncle Abe had become increasingly violent and destructive, and he scared away everyone who came to help him. So, my mom started staying with him to her detriment, and to the detriment of her marriage. Then, in 1992, I agreed to stay with him. It was the worst week of my young life, culminating in him spitting in my face and knocking me down as I tried to clean up a messy diaper.

After that, my mom basically moved in with Uncle Abe to help him. By that time, she had been laid off from her bank job as a casualty of one of those 80s-style hostile takeovers that were the stuff of cinema. At the same time, Uncle Abe's actual nephews, who lived across the country, were able to wrest his guardianship away from my mother to put him in a nursing home.

I want to be very honest: Uncle Abe belonged in a skilled nursing facility. Neither my mother, nor hired helpers, nor I were able to provide him with the kind of care he needed.

Did Uncle Abe agree? He might have been completely non-verbal by that point, but his feet still worked. He voted with his feet and escaped twice from the home before they figured out how to keep him from getting away. He also discovered a renewed desire for the ladies, and the staff had to figure out how to keep him out of one woman's room in particular.

The winter after he moved into the facility, Uncle Abe died. My mom, my dad and I were there holding his hands as he struggled to pass. He had no idea who we were, but with one of his last breaths, he sighed up to my mom, "Ah, Mama." And then he was gone.

I want to pause here to talk about how my family viewed

nursing homes. Thirty years ago, a nursing home was where you went to die. You didn't go there to live out your life. You went to a nursing home when you were too old or infirm to do anything other than lay down and exhale your last breath.

I recall my father weeping when he had to agree to the decision to put his grandfather in a nursing home, where he died weeks later. In my family, a nursing home meant death, and senior living communities weren't as popular or accessible as they are now.

As an aside, most of my family still feels this way. I think having seen the care my mom has received in her community has helped my own family understand that while nursing homes and medical rehabilitation clinics are filled with sick people who may or may not get better, a senior community, or a memory care community exists to give a senior as full and rich a life as they are capable of experiencing.

I know some members of my own family saw me as a traitorous child or as a failure because I didn't take my mom into my own home, but I see it like this: I have given my mom accessible housingthat is built specifically to accommodate her needs, with round the clock professional caregivers who know how to do all the medical things I am too squeamish for, and hot, healthy, really good meals that she would never get from me because she never taught me to cook. All she lacks is 24-hour access to me, and if anyone thinks their mother should have 24-hour access to them once they've flownthe nest, I have a really good therapist who can help them get over that feeling.

There was an assisted living community a couple of miles from our house where I volunteered as public service hours my senior year in high school. It was brighter and sunnier than Uncle Abe's eventual nursing home, but it was still cold and sad. I remember it smelled like canned green beans and sewage, and the people who lived there were like very well preserved zombies. (Side story: One of the ladies I visited with on my rounds often told me that her family had abandoned her. She was so sweet and soft, and I felt so sad that no one came to visit that I doted on her in my time there. I later discovered that she was the same beloved aunt that my mother's best friend was visiting every week. She just couldn't remember how many members of her large, loving family were visiting her each week, or how often.)

Uncle Abe's nursing home was an *American Horror Story*-looking nightmare of a place, with flickering fluorescent lighting and constant, thready wails echoing down the hallways like ghosts. It gave me the creeps, and it only served to strengthen my mother's resolve to never let her parents go to one.

My Grandparents

My grandfather had his first stroke in 1987, and we nearly lost him. He was the absolute love of my life, and seeing him as he recovered from first the stroke, then repair of an aneurysm was heartbreaking. With my mother at his side, he did recover and rebounded to a slower-moving, slightly impaired version of his former self.

He was well enough to drive from Georgia to Texas for my high school graduation in 1989, and managed along for several years before another stroke and heart disease took him down into a wheelchair. By 1998, it was clear that he needed more help than my grandmother and a regularly visiting cousin could give him, so my mother, uncle, and aunt worked together to move my grandparents into my mother's house.

I had moved back home to help her when my parents divorced, and I stayed to help her when my grandparents moved in. My grandmother, who suffered from macular degeneration, was rapidly losing her sight as my grandfather slipped further and further into the darkest corners of his mind with what I believe was vascular dementia brought on by his strokes.

My mother was committed to keeping my grandparents in her home to care for them. Very quickly it became clear that she could not run the small business she had worked so hard to build, and care for them at the same time. She sold her nutrition store she had loved so much and took a job working for the State of Texas, believing that the set hours would allow her to better care for them.

We hired a sitter to be with them during the hours she and I were both working, to take my grandmother out on errands, to help my grandfather with his bathroom needs, and to be company for them. During the day, my grandfather was no trouble, sitting quietly to watch TV, but as soon as the sun started to go down another man emerged.

At night, my grandfather suffered from Sundown and he became paranoid and fearful. He often believed he was on a battle-field in Korea, and he would scream from his bed, begging my grandmother, my mother, and me in turn to check on his men. He was worried his men didn't have blankets, or enough to eat.

At first, we all tried to comfort him that he was okay. He was in Texas, not Korea, and he wasn't in the Army. Soon, though, we realized that the right thing to do was to meet him where he was. "Your men are okay, Boom," I would tell him. "I checked them all. They are warm and fed, and they said thank you for the drinks."

Then, he would settle down for an hour, sometimes two before starting to scream again. We didn't get a whole lot of sleep while he was with us.

My mom's house wasn't built to be accessible by wheelchair, and frankly we destroyed it trying to make it fit my grandfather's needs. We tore out the carpet and left the concrete bare to make it easier to push his chair up and down the narrow hallway in the ranch-style home. We rigged safety bars in the master bathroom to help him pull up and ease himself down onto the toilet, blocking off the shower in doing so. We moved out and gave away furniture my mom loved because she loved her dad so much more, and she was not about to let him end up the way Uncle Abe had.

For the first few years, our weekends were spent driving hours to get to specialists who practiced on Saturdays. My mom didn't believe in Western medicine, so she hauled my grandparents two hours one-way every Saturday to see a particular chiropractor, who swore he could make my grandfather walk again. He didn't.

We made long day-trips out to see healing evangelists, who swore that faith in God would reverse all of the effects of my grand-father's strokes and old age, and magically restore him to the hale of his middle-age. They did not.

We also visited with D.O.s who prescribed actual medication to go along with the scores of vitamins and herbs my mother was giving my grandparents daily, after carefully reading lists of ingredi-ents and consulting textbooks to make sure nothing clashed, and no combinations would have bad effects. My mom poured her life and all her free time into my grandparents, gladly.

I hated it.

There. I said it. I hated it.

I hated spending my weekends driving to doctor appointments that weren't even with real doctors. I hated the false hope. I hated the constant busy work, the endless whirl of motion that my mother kept stirred up in order to combat her own feelings of helplessness.

Aging isn't a disease. Aging is normal. When you are eighty and you've had several strokes and heart attacks, it is normal that you have trouble walking. No amount of spine alignment is going to make you walk like you did when you were twenty. If you are a care-giver, it isn't your job to turn back time, or be a wizard. But my mom wanted to fix my grandparents. She wanted to be able to make them whole. She couldn't face her own helplessness or either of their mortality, so she just kept running on a hamster wheel of quackery that promised miracle cures.

She didn't understand that it was okay to walk into the end of my grandparents' lives with them, and walk alongside them as they came to the end. She wanted to give them immortality, and she tried to do it by sacrificing every free second of time, and every cell of her being. It was as though she thought if she could give enough of herself to them, they would magically be forty again. And, listen, if my grandmother could have sucked any amount of life out of my mother to extend her own, she'd have had a Slurpee straw down my mom's throat sucking away.

My mom damaged her own health in caring for them. She ignored her own check-ups and eschewed advice to have her blood-work done based on symptoms she showed, and her family history. She absolutely tore up her back trying to move my grandfather, lifting him when he fell, pulling him in and out of the car, and lifting and hauling his wheelchair.

She very literally gave them everything she had. She gave them her house, her finances, her thoughts, her time, her constant care, and her body. There was nothing left over for my mom.

While my grandfather was quiet and solid, my grandmother was mean and awful. She lied constantly to family about how abused and neglected she was. She called the police and reported neglect. She called the police and had them sticker my mother's car, saying it belonged to a stranger. She harassed my grandfather, my mother, and me regularly.

She hid things and said they were stolen. Here's a list I can remember off the top of my head:

- Spoons—she said the sitter was stealing our spoons
- My wedding invitations—she hid them under the sofa and didn't return them until after I had paid to print new ones
- My shoes—she thought if she took my shoes, I wouldn't leave the house
- The keys to the cars
- Food of all kinds
- Jewelry

This wasn't a matter of her moving something and thinking it was lost. This was a matter of her being an absolute gremlin. I loved that tiny gremlin with my whole heart, but she was, with her whole heart, shockingly mean.

She was diminished by age, by blindness, by being stuck in the house with an invalid and a low-paid worker, deprived of every freedom she had ever enjoyed from driving up to get a cup of coffee at Denny's to losing herself in a book. If she were alive today, I'd have her all set up with a subscription to Audible and regular Door-Dash deliveries of her favorite foods, but in the early 00s, all she had to look forward to was my mom or me coming home from work, and by the time we got home she was so sad and angry, all she could do was damage.

I pressed my mom to move my grandparents into an assisted living community. For a little over the last year of his life, my grandfather was bedfast. His world became a hospital bed in his bedroom, or, if we could get him up, he could sit in his wheelchair in the living room. We couldn't take him out, though. His world shrank down to nothing but a feeding tube.

By that time, I had moved out of the house again.

I need you to understand that my grandfather was the most gentle man I've ever known. He was a kind man. He was a solid man. He was honorable and dutiful, and he was someone you could trust with your life. As his mind slipped away, so did filters, and so did his ability to reason and control himself and his urges.

One night, I was reading to him, and he took my hand and tried to put it on his crotch. "Help me," he said.

I thought maybe he had an itch or needed to urinate. He grew more explicit, and he tried again to get my hand down on hiscrotch, while he asked me for a hand-job.

If he had been in his right mind, that never would have happened, but I believe dementia had robbed him of "right". I told my mom what happened and she flew into an absolute rage at my grandfather, taking him by the shoulders and shaking his frail body in his hospital bed. It was ugly. It was so ugly. My mom locked me out of the room while she punished him for what he had done, andI felt oppressive guilt for having even told her. He couldn't help it. He didn't know better. And my mom couldn't help what she was doing either, because she was so exhausted and so past the point of patience that she was on a hair-trigger for meltdowns.

I decided right then I had to leave. If my mom wanted to keep them in the house out of what I thought was a misguided sense of duty, that was her choice. That was her decision. I thought it was the wrong choice and a very bad decision. I told her that for the umpteenth time. She couldn't care for all my grandparents' needs, and both of them were absolutely miserable. She wasn't caring for her own needs, and she was miserable. I couldn't live in it and watch it, or actively participate in it anymore.

I moved out.

I visited regularly, and I still helped with appointments, but being able to sleep at night was better medicine than all the Echi- nacea my mother ever pumped into me. I was able to be a better helper because I wasn't living in the situation. I was also able to see just how much my mother had lost, and how broken she was.

My grandfather died in the hospital bed in that bedroom. My grandmother lived with my mother for another couple of years, with increasingly awful behavior until late in my pregnancy with my son. Then, so she could spend more time with me and my baby, my mother and aunt agreed that my grandmother should have a change of scenery. Grandma moved to live with my aunt in San Antonio, where she died from complications during surgery to replace a hip she fractured in a fall in 2005, just months after my baby was born.

My mom went to pieces after they were both gone, and almost immediately, the scaffolding of adrenaline that had been holding up her health crumbled.

As Uncle Abe's experience with the nursing home had cemented my mother's plan to keep her parents in her own care, their experience clarified to me that I was not cut out to be a caregiver and I solemnly swore (to myself) that if/when my mother needed care, I was going to find a nice home for her.

My Mom

My mom was born on an Army base in Arkansas in 1943, just before her father shipped out to the European theater in WWII. She was my grandmother's first baby, by all accounts fat and sassy, and adored by her grandparents and older cousins. When her brother was born two years later, she remembers being equally delighted and aggravated. Her sister came along in 1949, completing the family just before my grandfather was deployed into the Korean War.

    Mom's memories of her childhood are equal parts southern Americana of tree climbing and bottles of pop, and American Horror Story levels of abuse. In the Before Times, when her memory was sharp, she told hilarious, colorful stories about the paper route she and her brother ran for several years, glossing over the dark fact that even when they wanted to stop running the papers they could not because it was part of the family's survival income. She would show me photos of her in dance costumes at recitals, and tell me about how she was riding the city bus on her own to go to those lessons when she was four years old. She would point to other pictures and tell me about the people in them, casually mentioning that her paternal grandmother had tried to kill her twice, kicking her into an open fireplace once, and locking her and her mother in a bedroom another time that she needed emergency medical attention.

"Granny Young didn't like girls," she said with detached nonchalance, then told me another story about how Granny Young may or may not have purposefully led to one of my aunt's gruesome injuries.

My mom had no good memories of her mother. Not one. The few good things she had to say about Grandma always came with a caveat of how Grandma had ruined whatever small blessing she had bestowed. Grandma sewed her a beautiful dress, then told her she looked like a fat whore. That kind of thing. That dress hangs in my closet now. The waistband measures to fit a 20" waist.

Recently, I asked my mom what was her favorite memory of her father. She glowed as she talked for twenty-minutes about him. When she paused to just smile, I asked, "What's your favoritememory of Grandma?" She spat back with narrowed eyes, "Noth- ing!" So, I let that go.

On our many rides at night, Mom often talked about how Grandma's drinking affected her. She told me about physical, mental, and emotional abuse she had suffered at Grandma's hands. She told me about how she had been molested by a man in the backseat of a car as a young child, while my grandmother rode in the front seat with a man who was not her husband. She said that Grandma told that man he could take Mom home with him, and he had, but something stopped him before he raped her and he tookher back to her mother. She talked about how she worked to protect her siblings from it. I can only assume she succeeded because my uncle and aunt's memories of childhood don't include things my mother experienced.

I never understood why my mother worked so hard to take such good care of her mother, given her childhood and my grandmoth- er's meddling in her adult affairs, including how she had schemed against my parents' marriage. I especially did not understand it in light of what a gremlin my grandmother was in our present-tense.

Regardless of the past, my mother poured everything she had into caring for both her parents. Much like she had poured herself into me as a child, and then Uncle Abe when I was a teen and wouldn't accept her obsessive attention, she turned everything she was inside out to make my grandparents' lives as good as possible.

In 2015, when I was a cast member of the *Listen to Your Mother Austin* show, I read an essay I had written called, "My Son Hits Like a Girl." In it, I told the story of how rumors of my mother's high school baseball prowess caught the attention of a scout from the Cardinals. He had driven to Fort Benning to see Joe Young play and was devastated to find out Joe was actually Joan.

He told her that if she'd been a boy, he'd have signed her to their farm team on the spot, and apologized to her that she was a girl.

I love that story, and I hate that story. I'm so proud of what an amazing athlete my mother was, as a dancer, as a baseball player, even as a boxer, but my heart breaks for the disappointment she felt. "If you were a girl, you could be a nurse, or a secretary, or a teacher," she told me. "But you couldn't play ball."

Later, she would take over my son's private coaching and teach him to bat. The dad-coaches on his city league were astonished, wanting to know who had taught him to swing like that. One asked him if his father had done it, and my son cracked up laughing at the thought. "No, my grandma did!" He said.

I also shared how my mother had swallowed back the disappointment of having a grossly non-athletic daughter, and had worked incredibly hard to find what I was good at and try to culti- vate those strengths in me. My mom was an excellent coach as well as a world class player. She was also very damaged by her childhoodand was a bit of Dr. Jekyll and Mr. Hyde as a parent, reminding me that I was lucky because her parents abused her in worse ways asshe hurt me.

There is so much that I admire about my mom. She is fierce and fiery, solid and loyal, determined and driven. She was also resistant to the idea that she needed help filling the holes my grandmother had punched into her psyche, so fear and paranoia based on very real experience often meant those good traits twisted into aggression, obsession, and bullying. As her only child from a fragile and then broken marriage, and with all the normal issues a mother and daughter face, that meant I was the sole target for all her affection and all her fear.

It was complicated.

It *is* complicated.

In October of 2008, when my mother was recovering from colorectal cancer in my home, I realized two things: I was not a natural-born caregiver, and my mom was a double-fisted handful of impossible to please when she's ill. I already knew that last part. I had remembered that from my childhood. As for me, I do not like touching people's bodies. I especially do not like touching wet partsof people's bodies, or broken parts of people's bodies, or just skin ingeneral. I have to really like you to be willing to put my fingers on your skin when it's all whole like it is supposed to be. Please don't ask me to dress a wound. I'll do it, but I won't like it. My mother had a couple of really gruesome wounds to dress in some really wet parts of her body. It was unbelievably gross, and I realized I was notnearly as patient as I had believed.

In October of 2008, my son was three, my husband was working full time and going to school full time. I was also working astressful, full-time job, caring for my little family while working on my mental health, and then driving 1.5 hours every night ONE WAY to visit my mother in the hospital, until I brought her home after a series of events in the hospital nearly killed her.

I learned that I had the patience to be my son's mother or the patience to be my mother's caregiver, but I did not have enough for both–and that's probably the healthiest realization I've ever come to and it set me up for success in the following years. I don't feel bad about that. I have limits and I know what they are.

From 2008 through 2014, at intervals, I would ferry my mother to and from appointments in order to be the detail-keeper. I took her to the MRI appointment when she took three times the dosage of valium they had suggested and then behaved so cruelly and so badly that I chose not to connect with her for a couple of weeks after I was sure she was back to normal.

She needed the MRI because in a bout of what was increasingly erratic behavior, she had "playfully" charged my son like a bull, tripped, and busted open my front door with her head, pile-driving my then-seven-year-old into a flight of stairs. She hit the door so hard, it knocked out a chunk of drywall behind it. A couple of years later, while "playfully" grabbing at my son, she would trip, fall, andbreak her arm.

In 2014, when she had open-heart surgery, I reprised my role of caregiver both before and after her hospital stay, and was there when she went absolutely insane in the ICU for three days (ICU psychosis is a very real thing), biting, hitting, and threatening staff. I stayed at her house with her to help her settle in and it was pure, unadulterated misery for both of us. I couldn't do anything right for her, and she couldn't find any relief. My mom suffered every emotional side-effect associated with open-heart surgery, without the willingness to do anything the doctor or I asked her to do because after everything, she still didn't believe in Western medicine.

When we made our six week return to the surgeon, my mom (whose recovery had been arduous and unending) admitted that she had stopped taking all of the medication that had been prescribed after surgery because she didn't think she needed it, and I saw red. I sat through the surgeon berating me for not taking better care of her, and not making sure she was taking her medication (I would ask, she would say yes, that was that.) I sat through her truculent response to his insistence that she take her medicine. I made it halfway home before I lost my temper.

I was furious that I had spent so much time and expended so much emotional energy into her health, only to have her scoff and say she could cure herself with herbs. I was enraged that I had missed important things with my son so I could sit by her side whileshe recovered since she was just going to kill herself with a refusal to cooperate with the doctor after the fact. I was livid about all the pieces I had been forced to pick up before and after her surgery, and what all I'd had to give up and do just to make her home habitable for when she returned from the hospital. I had poured money, time, sweat, and a lot of tears into her health. All she had to do was take some pills.

Of course, it's much more complicated than that. It always is.

A transient ischemic attack (or, TIA), is what kicked off the ER visit that led to the heart surgery. Now, I know that a TIA can also kick off or kick up levels of vascular dementia. With the 20/20 vision of hindsight, I can see that in the weeks and months after the TIA, my mom's mental health was never the same. I can see thatshe honestly could not understand the importance of her medica- tion routine. I can see that the part of her mind that helped her plan for the future, and helped her reason was crippled. I can see that my mother's current diagnosis of vascular dementia probably got its start in 2014—maybe earlier.

All I knew then was that my mother knew she had Type 2 Diabetes and heart disease and she wasn't willing to do the work to manage either issue, and I had a child to raise and a marriage to foster. I had to work, and I had my own physical and mental health issues to deal with. So, unless she needed me for transportation due to anesthesia (colonoscopies twice a year) or wanted company at the doctor, I released her to her own healthcare. I worried, but I let go of responsibility.

Over the course of the next three years, I saw (but did not recognize) all the symptoms of dementia in my mother:

- Confusion
- Trouble paying attention and concentrating
- Reduced ability to organize thoughts or actions
- Decline in ability to analyze a situation, develop an effective plan and communicate that plan to others
- Difficulty deciding what to do next
- Problems with memory
- Restlessness and agitation

- Unsteady gait
- Sudden or frequent urge to urinate or inability to control passing urine
- Depression or apathy

A Momversation

The first COVID lockdowns happened while my mother was living on the first floor, backside of a memory care community. Since I couldn't visit with her in person, I would walk up to her window and knock. From March through late October 2020, that was how I communicated with my mother.

ME: *(rapping at my mother's window)*
 Mom: *(flinging open blinds and chattering like an angry squirrel as they go up)* I NEED YOU TO CONTACT BRYAN'S FATHER AND TELL HIM I WANT TO SUE! I'M GOING TO SUE THESE PEOPLE!
 Me: What for?
 Mom: THEY HAVEN'T BROUGHT ME MY DINNER YET! I AM NOT USED TO HAVING TO WAIT THIS LONG TO EAT! THEY NEED TO BRING ME FOOD! I'VE BEEN HELD IN HERE FOR 72 HOURS WITHOUT FOOD OR WATER!
 Me: Mom, it's just now 5:15PM I know you usually get dinner about 4:30, but they have to serve everyone in their rooms individually, and yours is the last room down the hall and, I was here yesterday and you were eating when I came up. Also, you have a sink with a faucet if you need water.

Mom: *I do?*
Me: *You do.*
Mom: *I ate yesterday?*
Me: *Yes, and you had breakfast and lunch today.*
Mom: *Well, it wasn't good! It wasn't worth calling food.*
Me: *And yet...*
Mom: *WELL! SOMEONE CALLED ME A WHORE!*
Me: *A worker or a resident?*
Mom: *A resident.*
Me: *So, hmm, you remember that you live in memory care?*
Mom: *I forgot that.*
Me: *You do, you live in memory care. And you are doing fine, but some of the other people who live here are very confused—not like you—and that resident must have been very confused.*
Mom: *I will knock her teeth out.*
Me: *Probably best not to do that. You don't want to hurt someone who is confused. By the way, how many masks do you have on?*
(She had on three masks. one on her forehead, and one around her neck like a feedbag, and one hanging from one ear.)
Mom: *Is that what these are? I had no idea.*

And then her dinner arrived and she told me to go home so she could eat.

But, her color was good, she didn't have a cough, her energy was high, her balance looked good, and she was supremely feisty, so that's all in favor of her health.

I STARTED SCOUTING senior living facilities because I was worried about my mom's house falling down around her, and her not being able to manage or maintain it (and also because I plan in advance like I'm playing chess with Death), and I started trying to convince my mom that she needed to move.

We fought a lot. A lot. Our usual daily communication dwindled because her behavior was so erratic and unsettling. She was not emotionally reliable, and I started pulling way back on the time she spent with my son because I felt like she was using him to fortify

Taking Away the Keys

herself. It wasn't healthy for him. She started asking him to lie for her, and that was the end of that. She thought I was mean and condescending. I thought she was stubborn and killing herself.

And that's where we were in September of 2017, when after three days of her not answering her phone, I went to her house and found her wandering around pantsless and weeping.

And that's the day I became my mother's keeper.

Looking back, my mom was exhibiting behaviors symptomatic of dementia as many as five years before the day I found her wandering around her house in that state of pantsless confusion, and hijacked her out of the three bedroom house of my childhood and into an independent senior living community.

My mom has always been a little…weird. Her behaviors have never followed any kind of norm, or been at all regimented. Her moods have always swung wildly between delight and despair. She has always been unusually paranoid. She has always been abnormally unpredictable, careless and scatter-brained, and sometimes frighteningly in denial of reality. It was all part of her charm, if you weren't living with it.

So, the night she called me from a stranger's phone because she had lost hers and then gotten lost in Dallas, I just chalked it up to my mom being her kooky, forgetful self. If she hadn't had my son with her, I wouldn't have given it another thought.

The stranger gave her directions to get home, and I met her at her house to pick up my son and take her a burner phone to useuntil we could retrieve or replace hers. She was as distressed as I'veever seen her.

Before we did anything else, I started dialing her phone to see if maybe it was just under or between the seats. We could hear it, which was great. But we couldn't see it. Finally, when Mom and I leaned into the same space, I realized it was coming from her. The call was coming from inside. Inside her blouse. It was in her bra.

We laughed, sort of. She was embarrassed and angry. I was worried and angry. And, we were both in denial that something was really wrong.

I told myself that maybe her chest area was still numb from the heart surgery she'd had the year before. Maybe that's why she couldn't feel the vibration that accompanied the sound? I mean, she'd always gotten lost while driving. Half of my childhood was my mother being lost and us having to stop and ask directions.

It was easy to ignore the problem because I didn't want to see it. The problem inconvenienced my life. It meant I had to have hard conversations with my mom about moving out of her house. It meant hard conversations were coming about whether her driving days were over. It meant confrontation about how she couldn't take my son out anymore, and inconvenience to me because she was my best babysitter. It meant hurting her feelings and insulting her sense of dignity. And, it meant confronting my own mortality.

The writing was on the wall, though, and I started trolling the internet for information about how to ease cranky seniors out of their homes into Homes. I narrowed my search from everywhere down to three potential places.

Then, on that awful September day, I went to her house to find her wandering through her hoarder's nest dressed in only a t-shirt. She was confused about what day of the week it was and why I was there, and I couldn't be sure the last time she'd eaten.

I took her to IHOP and fed her, which seemed to help clear up her head, then took her to my house, where she stayed until I moved her into the independent living community a mile away.

Since her official move-in date of October 31, 2017 and her official diagnosis of vascular dementia on November 13, 2017, I've learned a lot about elder care, independent versus assisted living, and memory care versus nursing homes. I've learned the differences between hospitalized rehab and skilled nursing rehab, geriatric psychiatric units versus geriatric behavior units, versus geriatric care. I've learned about Powers of Attorney and Medical Directives. I've sold my mom's house and researched the best way to save her money. I've also freaked out a lot about her money.

I've dealt with doctor's appointments, and insurance, and the Department of the Navy, and the IRS. We've been through multiple stays in the hospital, a stroke, surgery, and recovery. I've managed her friends and family, a full-time job, and a teenager, and perimenopause.

I've learned tricks to manage medication and mental illness, while trying to take care of my own physical and mental health. I've learned to do what is necessary and let the rest go. I learned to let the internet carry my load, and let my friends carry me.

Caregiving for Someone Who Abused You

Dementia surprises me on the regular. I meet aspects of my mother's personality that were previously hidden to me. We have conversations I don't think we ever could have had before, but now, I'm having those conversations with someone who cannot understand what they do or mean to me. And, I am having those conversations with someone who can't remember she was ever unkind to me.

It is true that my mother used to hit me.

"Don't you mean she spanked you?"

When I worked up enough nerve to tell someone, that's what they asked me. More than once. It was a rhetorical question. "Your mother loves you more than anything in the world. She would never hurt you. I'm sure you just mean she gave you a spanking."

I quit telling anyone. No one wanted to hear it.

It is also true that my mother loved me more than anything in the world.

So, it's weird. My mom doted on me, lived for me, adored me, and also beat the shit out of me on a regular basis. She did call it spanking, and she explained that I just had very fair skin and that's why I ended up with bruises and weals. It wasn't how hard she was hitting me, or with what. It was just that I was pale. It was normal. And face slapping and backhanding, well…I was sassy. If I learned to watch my mouth, I wouldn't have to worry about it.

She had this thing she did where she would do the "spanking" part, then she would make me sit in her lap and she would cuddle me and tell me how much she loved me. It became a ritual. Family remarked on it. "Look how much that little girl loves her mother."

When I was three, we lived in Colorado.

My mom tells this story and she laughs. I used to laugh with her because I thought I had to.

I wandered away from her in the fabric store in Cinderella City Mall. I remember being lost, but I knew the way to the store owned by one of our neighbors. I asked someone to take me to that store, and that's where she found me. Along the way, I lost my little blue sweater. It had a hood. A part of me still keens for that sweater–I really loved that sweater. I know where I left it. It was on the back of a chair.

I don't remember the part between my mom finding me, and my mom taking me into the restroom. I do remember how afraid I was when I realized she was angry. She carried a wooden spoon in her bag, just in case. I do remember trying to get under the sinks in the restroom.

Surreally, I remember the way the acoustics amplified my voice when I screamed. And, I remember two ladies rushing in and trying to stop her.

I remember her posture and the way her back looked when she got between those ladies and me, and I remember her threatening to flush one of them down the toilet if she didn't mind her own business.

I also remember worrying and crying more, and saying, "I'm okay! Leave her alone!"

The ladies left and my mother resumed, and finished "spanking" me.

My mom loved this story because she thought it was so funny that the other ladies ran away, and she loved that I had defended her against them.

Taking Away the Keys

I was three.

I was three, but I knew the anger really well. I was used to having my face slapped. I was used to being taken by the shoulders and shaken until my teeth rattled. I was used to being slung around and just generally hurt. And I was used to being cuddled and petted, and adored after the hurting stopped.

I was sitting in the activity room with my mom and she was telling me about how terribly everyone in the facility treated her. "No one likes me. And they are all mean to me. They push me and they pull me, and they won't let me go where I want to go."

One of the first things I learned was that you can't reason with dementia, so I just let her talk and didn't try to explain. She went on, her credibility dipping as she told me that my aunt had called her that morning to ask her to come fix her car, and how she had driven all the way to Alaska to do so. My aunt lives in San Antonio. She left Alaska when I was a toddler. Also, I knew they hadn't spoken in quite a while.

"I'm telling you, Lane, I am telling you. I'm going to hurt someone here." She veered swiftly away from a three-level parking garage in Juneau and back to the memory care—which she believed was a prison. "I'm just starting to realize how much…anger…I have inside of me."

"Just now?" I laughed.

It was like that time she told me she was mellow and easygoing and I nearly ran the car off the road laughing because those are the last two words anyone who's known my mother for more than five minutes would choose to describe her. Mellow. I'm laughing right now.

Suddenly, she was right there in the moment with me. For a second, her eyes cleared and she tilted her head and regarded me shrewdly. I picked my chin up from where it rested in my hand, and looked back at her.

Slowly, seriously, lucidly she said, "I have used that anger to hurt you. I have really hurt you with that anger, haven't I?"

"You did the best you could," I answered. I didn't want to upset her, but I couldn't deny it either.

"Oh, Sweetie. I am so sorry. I am so sorry. There is so much I would change."

"I know." I took her hand. "You did the best you could–and look! I turned out okay."

"You turned out more than okay. Oh, Girl, you are my heart. You are my world."

"I know."

"And these people here are so jealous of you," she snorted, and she was gone. Dementia regained possession of her and she shared her belief that her nurses were trying to drive a wedge between us because they were jealous of our relationship and wanted her to themselves.

I put my chin back in my hand and let dementia rattle on until she tired herself out.

The last time my mother hit me, I was fifteen. We were standing in the kitchen. We were disagreeing. She said something. I said, "Duh," and rolled my eyes. Next thing I knew, there was blood in my mouth and my glasses were on the floor.

My mother was abused as a child. She told me about it regularly. She gave me great detail about the whens, the hows, the whos of her abuse, and she told me how lucky I was that she only hurt me a little bit, when I deserved it. She told me how lucky I was that she never loaned me to other people to abuse. This, as she rocked me, stroking my head after she'd hurt me.

By the time I was three, I knew how badly my mother had been abused, and that I was lucky she loved me so much and only beat me a little bit.

I was lucky. She could have done me a lot worse. And, at least by over-sharing all that information, when I grew up and faced down the demons that were haunting me, I could understand why she wasn't able to win against the demons she'd been fighting.

She did the best she could.

I'm doing the best I can.

The best I can includes sometimes staying away. Maybe the best you can do is stay away. If no one has ever told you this before, you aren't responsible for caring for someone who hurt you. If you choose to care for someone, you are doing a kind thing, but it is not a requirement. There is no obligation for you to manage life for someone who abused you.

Not being a doctor or therapist, I obviously can't diagnose my mother, but I did live with her for a lot of years and experienced the brunt of her mental illness to the point that I feel fairly confident saying she has complex PTSD, Paranoid Personality Disorder (PPD) and Disorganized Attachment style due to gross abuse in her childhood, and Surrogate Spouse Syndrome.

Why do I think my mom has PPD? Well, because she'd told me that everyone is out to get her and out to get me for my entire life. She raised me to believe I could only trust her and my grandfather, that everyone else in our family and definitely everyone outside our family was out to destroy the two of us because they were so jealous of our bond to each other. That, and she has every one of the symptoms associated with it[1]:

- Doubt the commitment, loyalty, or trustworthiness of others, believing others are exploiting or deceiving them.
- Are reluctant to confide in others or reveal personal information because they are afraid the information will be used against them.
- Are unforgiving and hold grudges.
- Are hypersensitive and take criticism poorly.
- Read hidden meanings in the innocent remarks or casual looks of others.
- Perceive attacks on their character that are not apparent to others; they generally react with anger and are quick to retaliate.
- Have persistent suspicions, without reason, that their spouses or lovers are being unfaithful.
- Are generally cold and distant in their relationships with others, and might become controlling and jealous to avoid being betrayed.
- Cannot see their role in problems or conflicts, believing they are always right.

- Have difficulty relaxing.
- Are hostile, stubborn, and argumentative.
- Tend to develop negative stereotypes of others, especially those from different cultural groups.

When I was growing up, my Marine father was regularly deployed or working nights as a civilian. Nights that he wasn't home–and it is not exaggerating to say years at a time–my mother had a routine. She would put me in her bed, or send me to bed in her room (and no amount of argument would sway her, I had to sleep in her bed) then, when she was ready to go to bed, she would shut and lock the bedroom door, push a large chest of drawers as far as she could against the door, then interlock a folding sewing table between the door and the dresser for good measure.

Once we were barricaded inside, she would check the pistol, put it between the mattress and the box spring at the corner of her side of the bed, check under the bed, the *en suite* bathroom, and the closet, and then she would try to sleep.

I know that I sound like I am exaggerating and I am used to people not believing me when I tell them with what kind of regu- larity my mother would sit straight up in the middle of the night and hiss, "Don't move." She had heard a noise. She would sit like a statue until she heard another noise (there was always another noise), at which point she would rise and throw on her housecoat, pocket the pistol, unbarricade the door and tell me not to move or make a sound until she returned.

If I heard the gun, I was to call 9-1-1. I was not to come after her.

She would stalk the halls of the house, and then she would walk around the outside of the house. Snow. Rain. Sleet. Sun. My mother was like the US Postal Service. No weather kept her from her rounds. Surprisingly, she never found anything, save for that one time she almost shot my father, who had come home early from work one night and gone to sleep in my bed since he couldn't get in his own bedroom door.

Ironically, when I was nineteen and home alone during the day when my mother was in Georgia caring for her father, a group of men did break into our house. I ran them off with a tart, "Is there something I can help you with?" (Obviously not the whole story, but the important part is that they ran off.)

My mom needed constant validation and attention from me. She was co-dependent, traumatized, and was always looking around corners for a fight. When her stress levels were high, she would antagonize me, picking at me physically or teasing me until I cried, begged her to stop, or finally screamed for her to leave me alone. Then, she would punish me.

She didn't have healthy ways to cope with her feelings, so she would pick at me until she instigated a reason to explode at me. That was how she let off steam.

She also used me to absorb all of her hurts, forcing me to listen to her talk about her marriage problems, the issues in her sex life, the issues she had with her own mother and mother-in-law, my father's extramarital affairs, and every conspiracy she'd cooked up behind every one of the nice things anyone had ever done for her. Since I can remember, she would put me in the car and drive for literal hours just talking and crying.

As a young teen, I begged her to stop using me as a marriage counselor. She would ask me to tell her if she should get a divorce, or fantasize about shooting my dad's supposed girlfriends. When I cried and told her I couldn't listen anymore, she would cry and tell me she'd go crazy without someone to talk to, and she couldn't trust anyone else. She threatened to kill herself if I wouldn't listen.

So, I listened.

To all outward appearances, we were the perfect Mother/Daughter duo. All of our family and family friends believed my mother was an angel. They all told me regularly that I was the luckiest girl alive to have her. She bought me whatever I wanted, took me to all kinds of neat places, talked me up like a top-tier hype-man, and we looked like perfect best friends.

And while I was definitely spoiled and coddled, I was also living a very dark double life as my mother used me to absorb all of her pain. I wanted more than anything to break free of her, but she had convinced me that if I left—even to move to the next town over—she would die. So, when my father did finally leave her, I felt like I had no choice but to go be with, comfort, and protect her.

I went into therapy at fifteen, after faking a nervous breakdown to try to get my parents into counseling. A teacher at my school had returned after a mental hiatus and detailed her own slip into mental disrepair. I asked her a billion questions, then spent the next nine weeks "breaking down" until the school told my mother I needed help.

Relieved to be in an actual shrink's office, I explained why I was there, thinking he would applaud my psychotic parent trap techniques and have my mom and dad come for group therapy, only to be told that mentally healthy people don't pretend to be mentally unhealthy. He had me there.

When he did finally have my parents come in, I tried to explain to my mom that I couldn't be her marriage counselor, or her buddy, or her proxy into a second childhood, and my dad agreed. I hadn't realized he had noticed. Ultimately, my mom decided we had ganged up on her, and refused to go back. When my number of visits covered by insurance ran out, I stopped going.

I went into therapy again when I was twenty. I thought I was there to talk about my Daddy Issues, but it became clear quickly that my Mommy Issues were the real problem. My parents were splitting at that point and I felt disloyal talking about my mother, so I quit going.

In short, my mom was a bully. When I was in labor with my son, she was causing me so much stress, I asked her to leave the room. She cried, "There is no way I am leaving this room! If you force me out, I'll lay across the door like a goddamned dog! You treat me like a dog!"

And you know what? It was easier to just cry and let her stay because I only had energy to either get that baby out, or fight with her. And when my son popped out, she grabbed the scissors, short-cutting my husband, to whom the doctor had been trying to hand them, and cut the umbilical cord. When I said something to her about it later, she shrugged at me and said she deserved to get to do that because she had raised me.

At the same time, she also made sure I had meals, and sleep, and baby clothes, and diapers, and help, so I didn't understand how to stop the one and accept the other.

When my son was five years old, I went into therapy a third time. Once again, I thought I was going to be talking about onething and I ended up back on my mom. This time, I stuck it out, worked hard, and started taking steps to sever apron strings I shouldhave cut twenty years earlier.

At that time, my mother was calling me upwards of twelve times a day, screaming at me if I didn't take her calls. She would call my boss and tell my boss to have me call her when all she wanted was to hear my voice and say hi. She was showing up at my doorstep without calling, sometimes as early as 6AM. She was picking up myson from school or daycare without me knowing, only telling me once she had him. She was complicating my life in ways I couldn't even understand, and I was afraid it was going to trickle down to mychild.

By the time I ended that junket in therapy, I was down to answering two calls from my mother per week, refusing to let her hijack my day or my child, and I was confident that I was breaking the cycle of emotional abuse.

That was between the cancer and the open heart surgery, and thank god for it because I know I could not cope with my mother now had I not spent that time facing down my childhood and life as a young adult. I honestly don't know how I would deal with her.

In the past couple of years, my mother's increasing helplessness and attending neediness, clinginess, and anxious drowning-man grip have threatened my grasp on kindness and keeping of gentle hands. She has tried me in ways I know I have only been able to manage because of time in therapy.

Do unto others as you would have others do unto you. Man–I feel that as an adult who is trying to give patient care to a parent whose patience was best described as thin. I have had every oppor- tunity to do unto my mother as she did unto me.

So far, I have not given into the temptation, but I have to work against it. Old bitterness, and a Greek chorus of ghosts from my memories shove me toward cruelty like boys pushing their friend toward a fight. "Do it! Say it! She deserves it! Get her!"

I have forgiven, but forgetfulness is a challenge. I remember. I can't help but remember, and then I want to avenge myself. For a very real moment, I want to fight for the child who could not fend for herself.

But then I look at her. She's so small now, and I'm so big. She is so weak and frail, and I am so strong. I could break her. It would be easy to break her.

But, like I told my son when he was small, we don't hit. We don't hit with hands, and we don't hit with words.

So, I hand her over to professionally trained caregivers and I walk away.

My grandfather didn't have a father, and from all accounts, his mother did not care for him very well. He was the love of my life until he passed that torch to my husband, and our son came along. I've often wondered what he could have been if he'd had a loving family.

When I had my son, the goal I set for myself as a parent was to be the kind of mother to him that I thought my grandfather had deserved. I figured the best way to honor my grandfather was to treat my child the way I wish he had been treated. I wanted my son to have the chances my grandfather didn't have.

I wanted to parent into the past to make a better future.

My mom was grossly abused. Grossly. Shamefully abused. I have often wondered what she could have been if someone had protected and cherished her.

When I took over care for my mom, the goal I set for myself was to be the kind of mother I wish she'd had. Because, if she'd had that mother, my mother might have been able to resist those demons that always got the better of her.

I am parenting the moment to heal the past—hers and mine.

My Mom's House

As I've said, I pretty much hijacked my mother's life in 2017. Between the last of September and mid-October, with her active permission, I took over her finances, took over getting her moved into independent living, took over her healthcare, and started working on getting her house ready to sell.

It was a huge undertaking and I wasn't sure where to start, or how I was going to get it all done. I guess my first lesson in care-taking was that prioritization is key. You have to have your ducks ina row, or you'll lose your mind. My ducks look like the North Korean parade army.

My mother has suffered from untreated depression with manic swings for as long as I can remember. My mother's house, when I moved her out of it, hadn't been cleaned in three years. Prior to her heart surgery, I'm not sure how long it had been. While my mom was in the hospital, I cleaned out her house.

The more I cleaned, the angrier I got. I was mad at her and mad at myself. I should have been a better daughter, I thought, and I should have made sure her house was clean.

But, ask anyone in my family. We were not known for being neatniks.

I suffer from anxiety and depression. I also suffered from a syndrome that I don't know as having a name. It goes like this: My mom liked shopping. My mom treated her depression and anxiety by shopping. She felt guilty shopping for herself, so she shopped for me. My mother was extremely depressed and anxious, so we went out nearly every night and shopped.

We shopped so much that I had two bedrooms full of things. I could not fit all the things in my dressers and closets. My closets and dressers were stuffed to bursting, and I had clothes and things dripping from every flat space, and in mountainous piles on the floor. I honest-to-god had nowhere to put things. I could not put things away because I had no space.

And I was sad and anxious, and afraid. Fear was a huge part of my childhood and young adulthood. If my room was a mess, I figured if someone broke in, they would hurt themselves trying to get to me. My mental health issues were exacerbated by the inability to clear space, and I was being literally buried by the physical mani-festations of my mother's issues.

I figured this out when my son was born, and she and I both started doing the same thing to him. Then, I started the gut-wrenching process of cleaning up my act, which started with addressing my mental health. I was a mess, y'all. But I only had about thirty-seven years of mess to clean up at that point. My mom had sixty-five and also cancer, so… One thing at a time.

Anyway, as I was cleaning her house, I was furious that she hadn't ever addressed the mess. I was also so sad for her, and so ashamed that I had failed her as a daughter, but also frustrated by my own helplessness, and worried about her dying in the hospital–it was a lot.

When she came out of the hospital, I offered to hire someone to help her keep things clean and she refused. She wanted me to come clean it for her. I laughed at that. I was barely keeping up with my own cleaning. I hired Molly Maids to do the heavy lifting for me. I wanted to do the same for her.

But, mental health issues are dastards, and by the time I moved her out of her home three years later, it was piled just as high with

Taking Away the Keys

unopened boxes from Home Shopping Network, clothes, shoes, Coke bottles and water bottles, and three years' worth of unopened mail, as it had been when I'd cleaned it out before her heart surgery.

On my first trip over to start the process of clearing the house to clean it to sell, I just stood in the entryway and cried. It was overwhelming.

Then, I told myself to pull it together and just pick a place to start. Just do it. Eat the elephant one bite at a time.

I chose the mail and here's what I did:

- I cleared a little space in the floor.
- I gathered armfuls of mail until I had filled the space in the floor.
- I sat down beside the mail.
- I started making smaller piles.
- Bills
- Notices
- Official Business
- Junk
- Correspondence
- Once the piles were sorted, I got up and put all the junk and notices in a trash bag and took that to the curb.
- I sat back down and took the bills, sorting those out by type and if it was recurring
- Credit card
- Utility
- Insurance
- Medical
- Other

From there, I found the most recent of each individual type of bill. I took two of each bill and photographed every page with my phone, capturing:

- Account Number
- Pay To address

- Amount
- Statement of charges
- Website pay information

I also wrote this information down in a little notebook.

Then, I bagged up all the bills in a trash bag. I know I should have shredded them. I did not. I threw them away. Don't @ me. I don't care.

- I took pictures of insurance account information, then threw those things away.
- I wrote all insurance account information down in my notebook
- I skimmed through the postal dates on everything else. If it was more than 3 months old, it went in the trash. If it was newer, I looked at it.
- Then, I threw everything else away.

After I got home, I needed to decide how to address payments for the bills I'd found.

- I opened a credit card with the bank my mom used (I have always been a joint signer on her accounts.)
- I started online accounts for every bill that allowed me to do it.
- For every account I could, I set up an auto-pay to the credit card
- For the ones I could not, I set up an auto-pay from Mom's bank to the bill
- For the ones with different balances, I set myself phone alarm reminders to pay
- As I paid, I put a checkmark in my notebook.

It took me about four hours to get through the physical mail and another two hours to get everything set up to pay.

Then, I went online to the post office and had her mail forwarded to me.

By the end of the first week in November, my mom's finances were under control, and I was making a tiny amount of headway in her house. And that was great because by the end of that week, we were in the emergency room and my mother's blood pressure and blood sugar were both so high, they were afraid she was going to stroke out before they could get them down.

I had a new goal: Get Mom healthy. The house could wait.

A Momversation

My mother: (wearing a blue shirt as she describes a blue shirt with silver stars that someone stole from her)
  Me: (squinting at silver stars just visible on her back)
  Mom: (detailing the fight she had with another resident as the other woman walked away with her shirt)
  Me: Hey, can I stop you a sec?
  Mom: Sure?
  Me: I think your shirt is on backwards. Can we fix it?
  Mom: Oh! Yeah!
  We fix the shirt
  Me: (looking at the silver stars) Is this the shirt that was stolen?
  Mom: (considering the design now visible on her chest) Huh... I guess it is. I guess she gave it back.
  Me: I guess she did.

My Mom's Health

November 9, 2017, my son was diagnosed with strep throat and I breathed a sigh of relief. Since finding my mother, dazed and confused, I'd been trying to talk her into going to the doctor, and she had kept refusing. Having had my son coughing in her face for days, I finally had an excuse to drag her to the urgent care. She was not happy about it, but she agreed that if Thor had strep, he had probably given it to her.

The strep test came back negative, but after three different people (an RN, a PA, and an MD) had used two different blood pressure machines and one old-school hand-pump cuff to get a read from my mother's arm, we won a trip to the emergency room. We could have taken an ambulance if we'd wanted–that's how high Mom's blood pressure was. She refused.

Eight hours later, we were released from the ER with an armful of prescriptions and a referral to a GP for follow-up.

236/97

420

Those were the numbers I wrote down in my little notebook. I was carrying it with me by that point because whenever I thought of something I needed to do for my mother, I would write it down so I wouldn't forget.

Those were the readings for my mother's blood pressure and blood sugar when we got to the emergency room. They let us leave when they got her down to 130/82 and 236.

"I don't know what these numbers mean," I told the attending physician in the ER.

"They mean your mother is at high risk of stroke or death." "I'm not having a stroke!" My mother insisted, then started muttering about being healed in the name of Jesus.

The physician didn't quite ignore her, but clearly, I was the one to talk to. I got a long lecture on diabetes and heart disease, but not nearly long enough because at that point in my life all I knew about either was that you shouldn't have sugar with one, salt with the other, and both would kill you.

However, it was the first in a long line of doctors talking to me like I was an abusive pet owner, who had willfully ignored the health of my mother. I'd only gotten hold of her a few weeks prior! I'd barely gotten her to the urgent care! I knew she needed medical intervention, but you try moving a 285 lb woman anywhere she doesn't want to go.

I ignored the tone and just wrote notes in my book. I figured I'd need that for the follow-up with the office doctor.

My mom home and tucked in bed, I went home and started scouring the internet. I'm honestly surprised she hadn't stroked out or died. The internet was pretty sure it was impossible for her to be alive, much less mobile and communicative. So, I filled her prescriptions, bought her a day/night pill container and got to work getting her healthy.

The first step was a visit with the office doctor who expressed some surprise at the fact she had survived the ordeal. Thank goodness for strep, right? Another twenty-four hours at those levels and she probably would have died, he said.

I pulled out my little book and read him what I'd written, confirming the numbers I'd taken from urgent care to the ER, and the numbers the ER had sent us home with. I showed photos of the pill bottles to confirm medication and dosages, and dutifully wrote down everything he said.

When he asked me why my mother had not been on medication previously, I looked to her. She pretended not to see me. She studied the wall, her chin jutting out stubbornly. "She doesn't like medication," I told him. "I know she's had prescriptions for her heart, but she didn't want to take them. She takes...herbs."

He hummed and made a notation. "How long has she had diabetes?"

"Erm... Mom? Didn't Dr. Chang make that diagnosis?"

"He said I had it, but I don't."

I thought of all the banana splits and two liters she had consumed in defiance of Dr. Chang's declaration. She took licorice root, she said, and that was enough to balance her sugars. I felt my own blood pressure starting to rise.

I said to the doctor, "At least ten years. I think that's the last time she's had a regular doctor. He said she had diabetes, so she quit going to see him."

"I don't have it," my mother said, sullenly.

"Well, Mrs. M," the doctor said, "you actually do. That's probably what has led to a lot of your confusion. When your blood sugar is that high, and when your blood pressure is that high, it affects blood flow to your brain and makes it hard for you to think."

Her attitude turned on a dime. "Oh!" She gasped. "I didn't know that!"

"Yes, you did you old fart," I thought angrily. "You've told people that yourself!"

We left there with another prescription and referrals to three specialists.

"He doesn't know what he's talking about," my mother huffed as I fastened her seatbelt. "We need to go to the vitamin store."

My Mom's Medicine

My mother's obsession with health food started when I was about eight years old. I spent a lot of time in the hospital and doctor's offices as a child with upper respiratory illnesses, chronic bronchitis, and along with acid reflux, a weird condition that ended up in a medical journal as a migraine stomach. The doctor was really excited about it anyway.

My doctor was ready to prescribe adult strength pain killers for me, but my mom worried about the side effects. Rather than his treatment, she took me around to alternative health stores until someone suggested Aloe Vera juice to her. It did help relieve some of my pain, and certainly helped with the reflux, so for the next six years, she pumped me full of the stuff. She also discovered carob, which is the chocolate substitute they serve in hell, and astrology.

The bottom line was that penicillin was out, and Echinacea was in. M.D.s were out and chiropractors were in. If an M.D. said it to her, she let it glance off her brain, then told the chiropractor, who would sell her some Shaklee vitamins.

Then, my mom bought a nutrition store and became the vitamin lady she'd always wanted to be, and after that her pride was caught up in treating herself with vitamins, minerals and herbs so she could show her customers that all they needed was a little more B12 in their lives.

When I got her into actual care, her doctor told me that all the herbs she was taking had probably saved her life because he couldn't see any other reason she was walking. Was she brain damaged due to high blood pressure and diabetes? Oh yes. Was she dead? Not a bit! But the brain damage was very, very real.

Over the course of the weeks after she agreed to take her medicine, it became clear that my mom couldn't remember how tofollow a schedule. There was not enough Gingko Biloba in the world. I had already put alarms in her phone to tell her when to goto breakfast, lunch, and dinner, and I was afraid more alarms would confuse her.

After several failed trials, this is what I came up with thatworked:

First, on the advice of my cousin, I bought my mom an Alzheimer's Clock. This clock would show her the Day of the Week, the Date, the Time, and the Time of Day.

Next, I bought her a pill case that alarmed and chirped at her.

She was sure she could remember her morning medicine, so I put her nighttime pills in the case and set the alarm to go off at 8PM. I put the pill case in front of the clock. She would be able to look at the clock, see the Day, match it to the day on the pill case and medicate herself.

For her morning medicine, I took ziploc baggies and taped them at eye level to the cabinets above her kitchenette. I wrote on each bag: Day of the Week: MONDAY, Time of Day: MORNING. And,this worked really well until it didn't–so, for about a year once she got into the habit.

For us, the biggest problem was that my mom just hates taking medicine. She doesn't believe in it. We struggled for a long time until I lost my temper and asked her if she wanted to see my son graduate from high school. She said she did. I asked her if she still wanted him to come and visit her after school (she lived across the street from his middle school and he could walk over.) She saidshe did.

I told her if she didn't take her medicine, she would die before he made it to high school, and if she didn't take her medicine, I wasn't letting him come over alone because I didn't want him to be the one to find her cold, dead body. Whatever vascular dementia had already done to her brain, those words made it through the squeezed out blood vessels and she heard me.

And, until she just wasn't able to manage it for herself anymore, she took her medicine. Getting her to the appropriate doctor visits, though, that was another story.

A Momversation

Mom: Mr. Lundy has a hernia. I tried to tell his family I could put it back in, but they won't listen.
Me: Maybe because you aren't a doctor, Mom. Maybe they would like it if you left them to it.
Mom: I have put back in hundreds of hernias.
Me: Um...
Mom: Anyway, there is an old cowboy remedy. You drink a lot of water and jump from a bale of hay, and that pops it right back in. He could do that.
Me: Mr. Lundy is in a wheelchair and can't even stand unassisted. I have no idea why these people won't take your advice seriously.
Mom: It works. I wish they would just let me pop it back in for him.
Me: ...

I MAY HAVE MENTIONED that I have a full-time job. I have that job because we have a mortgage and a kid coming up on college- age. I don't have the luxury of not working and being a full-time caregiver, thank god. But, having a job also meant needing to find a way to get my mom to and from doctor appointments when I couldn't take time off to drive her myself.

We could have taken advantage of the independent living community's shuttle van, but my mom hated that, so instead I found a driver/sitter through care.com and hired her to pick my mom up, sit in the waiting room while she visited the doctor, then take her to lunch afterward.

For each different doctor, I called in advance with all her insurance information, talked to them after for instructions, and gave them my credit card for payment over the phone. It wasn't a perfect solution, but until she got really bad, it worked.

After her stroke and other emergencies took out the power grid in her brain, I had to be at the appointments with her. Then, I hadto start making decisions about which doctors really needed to be seen. She definitely needed to see the dermatologist because of the skin cancers, but we could hold off on the optometrist.

I felt bad making those value decisions. I still feel bad making those value decisions! But I remind myself that she wouldn't be going to any doctors if I weren't the one making the appointments, so I persevere.

People have asked me how I do it. How do I care for my mom while working full-time, raising a kid, wifing a husband, managing a house, and trying to have something left over for myself ? I just persevere.

There is nothing magical or easy about it. I just get up and do it. When I don't feel like doing it, I still get up and do it. When I'm anxious about it, I still go out and do it. When I'm angry about it, I shove down my feelings and do it. I eat the elephant one bite at a time, and sometimes I take a couple of Advil PMs, or I shoot some tequila just to go to sleep.

And I take good notes. Here are some basic notes for you.

For When You Take Over Someone's Life

Basic Organization

PAPERWORK NEEDED

REGARDLESS OF WHERE your Loved One (LO) is right now, if you know that you will be the main caregiver for them, you need the following in place as soon as possible. Scan these documents to a secure folder so that they are easy to access because you're going to need them a lot.

LEGAL DOCUMENTS

- A durable statutory Power of Attorney (POA)
- A HIPAA release
- A medical directive
- A medical Power of Attorney
- A will

The POA will allow you to make decisions for and sign for your LO. For example, if you are moving your LO into a care community, you can sign all the paperwork. The HIPAA release will allow you to get your LO's medical records, the medical POA allows you to have medical conversations and make medical decisions on their behalf, and the medical directive should be in place so that care staff and hospital staff understand how you and your LO wantthem to treat situations that might require heroic efforts (ie., if your LO is dying, do they want to be kept alive on machines, or do they want you to let them go?)

A will means cutting through months of red tape that might tie you up if your LO dies without naming a beneficiary.

You can go through an attorney to get all of this paperwork, or you can DIY the docs yourself online. My mom had all of the documents drawn up with an attorney prior to a surgery, so we had those in place well in advance of her deterioration. As a notary, I helped several caregivers officialize documentation for their LOs and themselves.

Do keep in mind that if you go the DIY route, you will need witnesses to attest for your notary statements. These witnesses cannot be people also signing the documents.

Identification Information

Start a file that includes all of the paperwork above and:

- Copies of your LO's driver's license/state ID,
- Passport
- Insurance cards
- Social Security card
- Any credit card or bills that they hold balances on
- Include account numbers
- Billing payment addresses
- Phone numbers for support or service

    A trick I learned was to laminate a color copy of my mom's ID and insurance cards, and give that to her, while I held onto the real thing. She went through seven lost wallets before I got her into memory care. One of those losses occurred the day before we were supposed to close on the sale of her house, and she needed her ID. More on that later.

    Also, take pictures of the fronts and backs of everything and keep them in a secure folder for easy access. You'll need this infor- mation more often than you think.

Medical Information

If your LO is under the care of a doctor, add this to your file:

- Doctor specialty
- Doctor name, address, phone number, email address
- Last visit information

Any time you visit a physician with your LO, they are going to ask you some questions. It's good to have this information handy:

- A list of your LO's family medical history
- A list of your LO's medical history
- Surgeries
- Diseases
- Hospital Stays
- Last vital signs at visit (Blood pressure, Blood sugar, weight, etc)
- Any medications
- Name
- Amount
- Pharmacy name, address, phone

Be prepared to spew out this information like you are expected to know your own name. You might want to print all this out and take it with you to every doctor appointment and just hand it over as part of your check-in. I keep a tiny notebook in my purse (and in my ER go-bag) with all that information written down, and at each doctor visit, I take new notes. You could probably do this on your mobile device, but I find that writing it down helped me hold onto the information better, and I could just hand the notebook to my partner when I couldn't make a visit.

Finances

Banking

I highly recommend a joint checking account. Whether you put anything in it to begin with is up to you, but once you are in control of your LOs finances, having their direct deposits like Social Security, or pension/retirement, or just their tax return going directly into an account you control will build back time into your life.

I opened a credit card specifically for my mom's expenses, tied to our joint account. That way, I pay all her bills through that card and then pay off the card monthly through her account. This means no auto pays have the potential to hit her account and wreak havoc with accidental overdrafts, and I get the bonus of reward points. I deserve every single point I get.

One thing we did as her memory declined and she started losing wallets all over the place was to get a pre-paid Visa card from her bank. I put a small amount of money on that card for her to use when her community went on outings, and to give her a sense of independence. But, when the card was lost, I could call the bank to cancel the card without worry that someone might have access to her checking or savings accounts, or might be running up charges on a real credit card.

Take pictures of the front and back of all cards so you have that information handy when you have to call to turn them off and ask for a replacement.

We went through seven of those cards. I found six of them when we moved Mom from independent living to memory care. I have no regrets.

A Momversation

Mom: You said you brought me hairspray. You didn't.
Me: It was in the little pouch bag.
Mom: You know they steal everything. This pouch is empty except for some pink lip balm that I know you would never buy me.
Me: I didn't put any lip balm in there, no. Hmm. Mom, when they delivered the pouch to you, you called me and you were really upset. Is it possible that you emptied the pouch and put the contents away, and maybe you put the lip balm in there? Can you look on top of your table and see if the hairspray is there?
Mom: I know they stole it. They stole all my clothes, too. And my phone. Me: (I didn't even bother about the phone) It's a big white bottle of Paul Mitchell. Do you see a big white bottle anywhere?
Mom: (long pause) Oh. I guess they put it back.
Me: I guess they did.
Mom: I'll have to hide it.
Me: NOOOO! You'll never find it again!
Mom: (cracks up laughing) Then you'll just have to buy me more.
...Later...
Me: (filling out a scholarship application)

Application: Why would you benefit from a scholarship?
Me: (considering the above) I keep having to replace my mother's glasses, toothbrushes, hairspray, and bibles every month?

Death Math

Senior care is expensive. There is no way around that. There is no sugar coating that. Price alone will make senior communities prohibitive for many families.

Hopefully, your Loved One was independently wealthy and has already paid upfront for at least a decade's worth of care, or your LO saved carefully so that when the time came, there was money put aside for their care. But maybe your LO is like my mom and they believed the televangelists, that if they sent every spare dime into their ministry, God would provide for them in their old age.

My mom had $10 in savings when I took over her finances, and that was only because when I had originally set up her accounts, I put a $10 monthly auto transfer on from checking into savings to avoid a service fee.

We are actually pretty fortunate because my mom worked for the state, so she earned a pension. It's not a lot, just around $600 a month, but it's more than nothing. Added together with her social security check and the monthly allotment she was awarded in her divorce, her monthly income covers about 2/3s of her memory care cost.

The rest of her care fees come out of the savings accrued when

I sold her house. Once all the fees were paid, and outstanding bills were paid off, she had about $70k left over. And that's where the Death Math kicked in. How many years can my mother afford to live?

Average private memory care pricing starts in $4000 per month range, for a shared suite. That is, two small bedrooms attached by a bathroom, with a small, shared living space. If you want your LO to have their own space, you'll be looking in the $5000 per month range for a studio apartment, and then into the $6000 per month range for a one bedroom.

When my mom and I started this journey, she was in Independent Living, where her rent was $2800 per month. We were tapping about $300 out of savings every four weeks for rent. We were also tapping out between $500 to $700 on miscellany.

My mom had a lot of doctors' appointments and I had a full time job. So, I used care.com to find a geriatric babysitter/dri-ver/doctor-office-note-taker, who cost $25 an hour when I added in her tip. Worth every penny to keep me from being written up for excessive absences, at my job that paid less than $25 per hour.

Mom wanted to go out to eat with the ladies at her community and that was an expense. She wanted her refrigerator stocked, another expense. I had to pay movers to get her into the community, pay specialists to help me get her house cleaned and in shape to sell, and shortly after she moved in it became clear she couldn't do her own laundry anymore, so we were paying for that service as well.

I knew that memory care was looming, so I had the conversation with my mother. No, I couldn't keep her fridge stocked with food we were just going to throw away because she felt safer just having it in there. No, we couldn't afford to buy her cases and cases of Smart water anymore. No, we couldn't be spending $150 a pop on two packs of underwear from Catherine's every couple of months that she was just going to throw away after an accident. No, no, no. She cried. I held her hand and let her feel the feelings as I snatched away everything she loved.

Then, I went and sat in my car and I cried.

Death Math works like this: If Lane's Mom has $70,000 in

savings, and her monthly income is $2500, and her monthly expenses are $3500, how many years can Lane's Mom afford to live before Lane has to take a second job to keep her in care?

3500-2500=1000

70,000/1000=70

70/12=5.83

Lane's Mom can afford to live for 5.83 years before Lane has to take a second job to keep her in care.

And that was just if we kept her where she was.

She lived in Independent living for a year before a stroke took her down. While she was in recovery and rehab, I signed the paperwork to move her into assisted living. It was clear that she wasn't going to be able to go back to her apartment, but I was able to negotiate a deal on a really cute studio in a quiet community with a view of a winery and its vineyards.

All costs accounted for, we would be spending $4100 a month for Mom's care. I did have to pay for movers again, and I had to buy her a new little sofa because the furniture she had moved with originally was all but destroyed. The Death Math wasn't looking good.

Then, the day we brought her into assisted living, she went back into the hospital for six weeks, and came home to memory care at a whopping $5200 per month. The Death Math was gruesome.

But I found a different memory care community who was giving cut rate pricing due to losses they'd experienced during COVID, and salvaged some of the Death Math by getting her to $4000 per month.

I currently pay out of pocket for her personal expenses, like adult diapers ($60 per month), wipes ($35 per month), outings and treats ($200 per month). As of today, my mom can afford to live for 3 more years before I have to make significant changes in my own life.

My son will start college in two years, so I'm a little stressed. I am also a little resentful, to be honest. My mom's choices will mean that I am not able to save as much into my future, which means my son may be faced with the same dilemma I am one day.

There is a second chapter to Death Math. Finances are Death

Math I. Caregiving Clock Hours are Death Math II. It looks like this:

If Lane has a job with twenty days of PTO, a child who will need a minimum of 3 doctor visits during the year, and a mother who will need upward of thirty days of in-person care due to emer- gencies, hospital stays, doctor visits, follow-ups, specialist visits, andbecause she called and lied for attention, how quickly will Lane's boss decide he should hire someone else?

Death Math II also covers problems like:

If Lane's Mom has a doctor's appointment at 9am, and Lane needs to be at her job thirty minutes away at noon, what does Lane need to do to make that happen?

- Lane needs 4 bottles of water, 2 protein shakes, and 3 protein bars
- Lane needs a two hour lead time
- One hour to call until Mom wakes up
- Thirty minutes to badger her out of her apartment, luring with a protein shake
- Fifteen minutes to get her into the car with her walker, luring with a bottle of water and a protein bar
- Fifteen minutes to get her out of the car into her appointment
- Lane needs to be prepared to feed her mom snacks and hand over another bottle of water while they wait for the doctor because her mother regresses in waiting rooms and acts like she's a very spoiled five year old
- Lane needs for the doctor to be on time this time
- When the doctor is late, Lane needs to be able to calculate when she has to call her boss
- If the appointment ends at 10:30, we're golden
- If the appointment ends at 10:45, we can possibly make it
- If the appointment ends at 11, we need to call and say we might be about 5 minutes late

Taking Away the Keys

- If the appointment ends later than that, we sit in our car and we cry
- When the visit is over, Lane needs to explain to her mother, yet again, that no, they cannot go have lunch because Lane has a job, and no they cannot go to a drive-thru for the same reason
- Lane will hand over the second protein shake
- Lane will hand over any remaining protein bars
- Lane will find a mostly clean napkin in the console of her car so that her mom can dry her eyes while she's crying that she never gets to go anywhere
- Somewhere in there, Lane needs to find fifteen minutes to take her mother to the bathroom, thirty minutes to go several times if it's one of those days
- Lane is so tense just thinking about how hard it is to get her mom back into her community, that she's decided to include hours taken off her life by stress into the Death Math.

Caregiving takes a toll on your health. Whether you are doing it full-time in your home, or you are the decision-maker for an LO in managed care, it drains your battery like an app constantly running in the background. It's always there. It's always on. You are never fully relaxed.

This is the Death Math of science. 30% of caregivers die before the people they care for. Depression and auto-immune diseases are high on the list of reasons for caregiver death because caregivers often have to put off their own appointments and health management to take care of their LO.

One of the reasons I chose to put my mother into managed care was because I watched her wreck her body and destroy her health taking care of my grandparents. I was old enough to take care of myself, and did, but could not persuade her to take time for her own health and body.

My son is not old enough to care for himself. If I'm dead or disabled, he's going to have a rough time. So, I have started taking my own healthcare much more seriously. That's one of the reasons I always take a week off from visiting my mom every month. I need time to recharge, go to my own appointments, and just live.

You can't take care of your LO if you are dead. And, your LO probably wouldn't be making/keeping all of these appointments for themselves if you weren't the brains behind the operation. Take a step back and make sure you are healthy, you have yearly labs, and you're taking care of your eyes, your teeth, and your mental health. It will cost too much if you don't.

The People In Your Neighborhood

The People in Your Neighborhood

You're going to need help and support, and the broader your network, the better off you will be. Along with your doctors and your lawyers, you might find useful:

- A banker
- A trusted realtor
- A senior-move specialist
- A social worker
- Home health professionals
- A therapist—for you

Realtor

If your Loved One has property, you can go a few different ways with it. You can rent that out as recurring income to help fund your LO's stay in managed care, you can sell it, or you can hang onto it. In any event, a trusted realtor will be able to help you establish the value of the property and help you if you want to rent or sell it.

Personally, my husband and I have used our first home as rental property when the market was too slow to sell it. We have had good tenants and we have had SWAT teams kick in our door to arrest tenants. I highly recommend avoiding the latter.

We've also worked with a stellar property manager, and a property manager who rented our house to a guy who had federal warrants. So...

When we were ready to sell, we asked around and I got a personal reference from a friend. That realtor, Chastin Miles, became my realtor. He helped us understand how to get that house into shape for the best sale, then sold it in a week. Then he helped us buy a house. Then, when it was time to consider my mom's place, he got me through the entire process easily.

Chastin told me what he thought the property was worth, and I told him the bare minimum I needed to get out of it in order to keep my mom in Pampers. He found an investor and got us $20,000 more than we had thought possible.

A Senior Move Specialist

A Senior Move Specialist

My mom's house was in really bad shape. You couldn't walk through it easily, and there was no way to tell what was valuable and what was trash. The formal dining room/living room was full of unopened boxes of things she had bought from the home shopping network. Mail was piled up in stacks two feet high. The bathrooms were...rough.

I went over every weekend for six weeks and I wasn't even making a dent, so I started researching. I was Googling for people who helped in hoarding situations, and kept coming up with companies like Junktossers and Clutterkillers—companies that sounded like they might come in and maybe judge my mom harshly, or treat her things badly.

Finally, I found Settle In Solutions. Anne Barron came into my mom's home with a team and they sorted everything into groups: Valuable/Precious, Important Paperwork, Keep, Donate, Throw Away.

I had told Anne some of the things I was looking for, like my mom's divorce papers, the Power of Attorney documents, and her tax returns. She found them and set them aside for me.

Once the groups were made, I came in and gave my blessing. Then, Anne and her team cleaned the house beautifully so I could turn it over to Chastin.

We've used Anne's services twice since, when I've moved my mom. Anne comes in with her team and packs up my mom's apartment, then moves her things to her new space and manages all the interior decoration. Then, when my mom gets to her new apart- ment, it looks as much like the old one as possible, with her most precious things visible and her space easily accessible.

Anne's work has made my mom's transitions easier, and she's made her spaces so beautiful that other residents always want to be in my mom's pretty, peaceful rooms.

One other thing Anne helped with was me. I had horrible guilt over downsizing my mom from a 3/2/2 ranch style home into a 420 sq ft apartment. I was trying to find a way to take everything. Anne helped me understand how it was better to pick out the precious and make a simple space, rather than overwhelm my mom with the clutter we both thought she needed to be happy.

While I'm thinking about it, get some pepper spray. While I was working to clear out my mom's house alone, two different, strange men, at two different times just walked into the house unannounced and uninvited. One came back three times. Each time they were making demands to know about when the house was going on the market and wanted my phone number so they could buy it first. One was very aggressive and made me feel unsafe until I was able to get him out the door.

I wish I'd had pepper spray.

Banker

Banker

I was a licensed banker for years and years, so I had established relationships with branch managers and bankers across North Texas. That made it a lot easier for me when I started managing my mom's money.

As simple as online banking has made things, many people never set foot into a branch anymore, but when it's time to file your Power of Attorney over your LO's finances or be added on as a signer to their accounts, you'll need to do that. My mother had also been in banking, so many things we had done ahead of time as "justin case" precautions. Anything she thought I might need to access in an emergency, she added me onto as a signer.

- I was a co-signer on all her accounts
- I was a signer on her safe deposit box
- I was an authorized user on all her credit cards

Call ahead and schedule an appointment. Let the banker know that you want to establish a relationship to help manage your LO's finances. They may try to sell you investment services—do not bite on that immediately.

If you're just getting started here, keep your LO's funds as liquid and easy to access as possible. You can always schedule an appointment with an investment banker to build out or add to your LO's portfolio, but once you've committed funds to an investment account, they're really hard to get out.

A Momversation

Ring Ring

Me: Hello

Mom: Hi! What are you doing? Where are you?

Me: I'm at home working. How about you?

Mom: (sarcastically) Oh, I'm just sitting out here in this PLACE with these PEOPLE playing with some stupid thing that is supposed to make my mind WONDERFUL.

Me: Oh...

Mom: Some stupid animated seal that goes RO RO RO ROOOO and then you pass it to someone ELSE and they fuss, "Don't just hand it around, wash your hands before you play with it," and THAT is why I don't play with YOUR NASTY SEAL!

Me: I feel like you aren't trying to communicate that message to me, so much as to someone else.

Mom: I don't want to touch your SEAL!

Me: I'm sorry you had to play with a seal.

Mom: Oh, I didn't. I'm just sitting here watching other people blubber. Hmph. Maybe that's my problem. I'm missing a blubber button.

Me: Er...maybe we could get you one.

Mom: Hmph! No. I don't want one. I DO NOT WANT TO BE LIKE THESE BLUBBERING PEOPLE. Anyway, I just wanted to call you while my phone worked. I have to go now. BYE!

And I just let out a long breath and thank god for patient people who don't pick that seal up by the tail and whack her with it.

A Social Worker

I really lucked out because one of my dearest friends has worked for The Senior Source of Greater Dallas since her undergraduate internship, and my cousin has spent her progressively responsible career in adult daycare. When I started down this road with my mom, I peppered them with questions. You might not know anyone personally, but a quick Google search will help you find the help you need.

I asked my favorite social worker, Renae Perry, LMSW, COO of The Senior Source a few questions that I thought might help us all. Here is what she had to say:

Q: The Senior Source is great if you are in Dallas. Do you know of any national resources YOU would recommend that can help people in other locations?

A: There are a few ways folks could find out about helpful resources in their local communities. 211 is a national resource number that covers all fifty states and serves as an information and referral number. You could call and ask about caregiving or aging related resources in a particular area. There is also an Area Agency on Aging for every county across the country, and someone could look up the contact info for the county they live in. These AAAs often have respite services for those who might not be able to afford private respite care, as well as be able to speak to other organiza- tions that serve and assist family caregivers.

For anyone with a loved one in a nursing home or licensed assisted living facility, the Long-Term Care Ombudsman is a resource I strongly recommend. There is an ombudsman for every county across the country. They advocate for quality of care and life for residents in these facilities and address complaints and concerns. They can also be a helpful resource to families and individuals in the process of choosing a long-term care facility. They aren't able to make recommendations, but they can help narrow the list, share concerns at particular facilities, pull up the state's licensing informa- tion and go over any deficiencies or issues sited with families.

Disease-specific national organizations can also be very helpful with support groups and information relevant to the unique chal- lenges of caring for someone with a specific diagnosis. Alzheimer's Association, American Cancer Society, Arthritis Foundation, etc.

Q: What do you see as the most overlooked aspect of elder care?

A: Two things come to mind as I initially think about this question. One, caregiving for an aging loved one often happens suddenly. For example, an adult child might know that they will be caring for Mom or Dad someday, but don't see it as an immediate need. Then, there's an event - a fall, a stroke, etc - and suddenly there are, in many cases, immediate and significant caregiving needs and expec- tations. This can be overwhelming and made even harder if that adult child doesn't know what Mom or Dad wanted regarding care (if they lack capacity to share that now) and they don't know specifics of long-term care insurance policies, accounts, healthcare coverage, etc, or even what is important to that person regarding their wishes.

There's "the talk" with children about life issues that we all know about, but there's also "the talk" to have with parents and loved ones about their wishes and care needs before it's needed, so that adult children can be prepared, know where documents are, and know what their loved ones value in how they want to be cared for in their later years and as they decline. The Conversation Project is a great resource for how to have that talk and things to ask: https://theconversationproject.org/

So, to the degree that advanced preparation can occur, the better for all involved. It's usually an emotional time, so it's harder to think through some of these things in the moment. It can also be very challenging if there are siblings and they don't agree on what Mom or Dad would want. That advanced preparation can help with adult children being on the same page.

Where there's not consensus, it can sometime be helpful for an outside expert to come in and facilitate a group discussion, create an action plan and/or take over some of the management of care, so that the adult children can focus on being son or daughter. The Aging Life Care Association is a resource to find aging life care managers, aka Geriatric Care Managers, that can be helpful in situ- ations like this or when families have resources to pay for this type of support.

The second thing that often gets overlooked is self-care for that family caregiver. She or he (but it's more often a she) may neglect her own doctor's appointments, care needs, physical, emotional, spiritual, mental health needs in the all-consuming task of caring for that loved one. It's so important, though, especially if caregiving is going to last for a longer period of time.

Support groups can be helpful to develop relationships with others who understand what you are going through and can share tips and resources with each other. Respite care is important if the person is living with you. Having someone else available even for a short time to relieve you so that you can get a break is critical. There are several mindfulness apps or resources for caregivers that can be helpful here, as well. Think about what you do as a caregiver to relieve stress - if nothing comes to mind, find something or talk to a professional to help build in stress reducing activities in your day. Hobbies, exercise, reading, etc.

Q: If a person is dealing with care for a loved one who is in a different state, what do you think are the top five things they would need to do on a recurring basis?

A: We see this fairly often and it can be incredibly challenging.

1. If you can visit regularly and see how that person is functioning (if they are still living at home, especially), that helps you see when/if that person is declining physically or cognitively. Technology can be your friend here, especially with all of the options now for remote access - you can help track medication to making sure the stove is turned off - it can be very helpful, if you have to means to purchase.
2. As that person declines, it really becomes important to have someone locally to support them and ensure their needs are being met. Mentioned earlier, Aging Life or Geriatric Care managers can provide this type of support.
3. If the person is in a long-term care facility, get to know the staff and the ombudsman for that facility. Technology can also be helpful in video chatting that loved one - not to say there aren't challenges - you of all people know how challenging using technology is with someone with cognitive challenges!
4. Ensure all financial, medical documents are accessible. Having a local POA/medical POA is helpful if it's an option. If that's not an option, make sure you are part of medical checkups virtually (be on the phone with the doctor/nurse, etc) and you are regularly reviewing documents, accounts, etc.
5. Recognize that your loved one may be particularly vulnerable to frauds and scams, especially if there is any cognitive decline. So regularly check financial information and review who else is talking to that person.

Q: What do you wish people knew about elder care?

A: As isolating as it can be, there are resources to support and assist caregivers. Connect with those resources and/or others who know what you are going through and can support you. There's no such thing as perfect - doing the best you can in that moment is okay. There can be a lot of complex family dynamics at play in caregivingfor parents - you don't ever actually become your parent's parent - they are still the parent even when you are providing for their most basic needs. There are lots of emotions with that. Be gentle with yourself and how those feelings show up. Preparation and frequent conversations before caregiving is significant and can be very helpful.

The Internet

The week before we were set to close on the sale of Mom's house, I was out of town on business. I was scheduled to get home on a Sunday night, and we were to go to closing on Monday morning. Mom called me on Wednesday and said, "I lost my wallet." It was the third one in as many months, and I had made the rookie mistake of giving her actual ID to her. I had a photocopy of it, but she'd seemed so lucid that I'd felt confident she was on the mend and wouldn't lose another wallet. Wishful thinking.

Without her ID, we weren't going to be able to close on the house. I got online from my phone and used the copy of her ID to pull the necessary information to order her a new ID, giving me a paper ID and a photocopy of the actual ID to take to closing along with an expired ID that I still had in my possession from the first time I had to order her a new card and found the old one. (Andthen I called all the places she said she had been because her social security card and $500 cash were in that wallet. This was early dayswhen I really thought Mom might recover and was second guessing a lot of my choices. Later, I found the wallet hidden inside a sock, wrapped in three pairs of underwear, tucked securely in her night- stand. That's totally normal behavior.)

Having access to the internet saved my life. With a job, a family, friends, and pets to care for, I was doing good to shop for my own groceries, much less my mom's frequent and random grocery needs. The more of her life I took over, the more I found myself relying on the internet. Here are some of the sites I frequented.

- Instacart – They deliver directly to the door. I could get my mom's groceries or weird wants delivered to her, when I was an hour away at work. She didn't have to suffer so much for lack of her own wheels. Now that she's in memory care, I still use Instacart to deliver emergency replenishments of things like adult diapers and wipes, or the occasional treat. I leave a note for the driver to text me the name of the admin at the desk, so if Mom doesn't get her package, I know who to ask.
- Care.com – I hired driver/sitters for Mom from care.com. She needed someone to take her to dentist appointments, or the eye doctor, or the dermatologist and I couldn't take the time off work, so I hired a lady to pick Mom up from her community and drive her, sit in with her, then take her to lunch. It took three tries to find a lady Mom liked, but then we worked with her for six months, until Mom had a stroke and needed me to be present at every appointment. I also used Care.com to hire someone to visit with Mom and take her shopping, but she hated that.
- Uber Eats/DoorDash/GrubHub – When Mom was in independent living, she regularly wanted food other than what was served in the dining room. I couldn't be at her beck and call, but Uber Eats could! And I could pay for it and manage the tipping, and she didn't have to try to figure out the difference between a dollar and a post-it note. She tried to pay someone with post-it notes, once.
- Aplaceformom.com and caring.com – When I was searching for communities for Mom, I worked with both of these groups to find the best options available within

Taking Away the Keys

our price range. They even scheduled the tour visits for me.
- Online banking and bill pay – This is the best invention! I could manage all of Mom's finances and bills from anywhere with an internet connection.
- Amazon.com Subscription Services– My mom needs certain things with regularity. I do not have the flex time to keep up with the shopping, so I have subscriptions for adult diapers, wipes, toilet paper, and toiletry items through Amazon.com. Mom gets regular shipments of all the things she needs to stay clean and fresh. If she runs out between shipments, I hit the Instacart app.
- Facebook Support Groups – Sometimes, you just need to know other people understand, but many times I've found important, actionable information in these groups. I've always found grace and kindness there.

Senior Community Living

Senior Community Living
I am a planner and a worrier. Or, I am a planner because I am a worrier. When I was in banking, I had to go to a lot of Chamber of Commerce meetings and business networking events, trying to drum up business for my branch. At the time, I was there to sell bank accounts. In hindsight, I see how lucky I was to learn about so many different businesses.

One event I went to was sponsored by an independent living community. I had no idea what that was, but I chatted with the marketing rep for a while and decided to win their business. I'd found a niche in selling business accounts to daycares, so I figured I'd hit the other end of the spectrum and make a niche out ofselling business accounts to old folks homes. Along the way, Ilearned some different terminologies, did some onsite visits to find out about business needs, and accidentally learned a lot about an industry that would be serving me and my family in about ten years.In any case, once I learned about senior living, I started planning.

My mom had surgery to remove cancer from her colon, and her lengthy convalescence in my home made it clear to me that she was never going to be able to live with us long-term. I am so proud of my friends who are able to be the personal caregivers for their LOs. That takes a kind of strength and patience I lack. Or, it takes a kind of person that my mother is not.

That in mind, I did some light research into the types of places that might be available to her, if I could ever convince her to sell the house that was crumbling around her and move into something manageable.

There is a lot of variety available, depending on your LOs level of need.

A Momversation

My mom goes through phases where she will call me fifteen times a day, or ignore me for days. We're in an "ignore" phase. Since she's wasn't answering my calls, I called up to the community to check on her.

Last week, they called me and reported that she had fallen, so I called her doctor, who has been out twice since Saturday, once to do x-rays. She twisted an ankle that has been bothering her for a decade, and the last time we talked, she was telling me about it.

Said the mother: My ankle is broken. I talked to the people who took the pictures and they told me it was fractured. And! They told me I wasn't crazy! That I knew all the words about what was going on down there, and that I knew exactly what was happening! They said they could trust me to know! AndI told them what that thing down there was called and they said they'd never seena fracture like that in the really long one of those.

Said the doctor: Ankle is swollen, but not sprained. No fractures or breaks. Keeping an eye on the swelling, but no need to boot. (I asked about that)

Said her charge nurse and the lead attendant: Oh, goodness. You know how your mother is. She's refusing to use her walker, so she limps. We tried to tell her that her foot is not broken, but she believes it is. You know how she is when she believes something. She is okay! She is good! In the mornings, she is very happy, in the evenings she is very confused. We just have to get her to use her walker again.

And I laughed because that is 100% my mother. If she uses her walker, she won't limp as much, and she's bound and determined to show them her ankle is broken, so by god she is going to hobble around until they agree with her.

55+ or Senior Living Communities

These are places that exclude residents under a certain age, usually around fifty-five. These range from apartment complexes, condos, and townhouses, to McMansions in planned neighborhoods.

In general, these communities offer a kid-free living experience, centered around activities that we have come to associate with the Olds. Rather than having to worry about twenty-somethings throwing a party outside your apartment door, of a family with screaming toddlers closing down your pool area after a potty acci- dent, residents can expect a more peaceful world.

Some of these communities plan outings and vacations residents can enjoy for a group fee. I worked with one group that used to take a bus full of seniors to the casinos in the next state for weekends at a time, and set up fishing excursions in the Gulf of Mexico for any interested residents.

While there may be concierge services available, this is a place for people who are perfectly fine living on their own. This is for people who want to downsize, ditch lawn maintenance, or just get away from youthful exuberance.

- What you pay for: Your domicile and potential HOA or Community fees.
- What's extra: Outings and other concierge services
- What you don't get: Medical care, Medicine maintenance

Independent Living

For people who want to live on their own, but don't want to bother with house maintenance or the cooking and washing up anymore, independent living is a good start.

In an independent living community, you retain your autonomy and you're on your own schedule unless you want to take your meals in the community dining room.

Generally, independent living offers three meals a day as part of your monthly rental payment. They may offer snacks between meals, or special amenities like coffee or juice bars. Should you choose to partake, your meals are served restaurant-style or can be sent up to your apartment as room service.

These communities plan activities and outings for residents, host events and church services, and are similar to 55+ living, save that these communities are often more secure. Think of them like a big hotel, where after hours, you need a code to get in the front door. They also usually provide residents with panic buttons in theirhomes, and panic pendants to wear for emergency service.

The apartments usually include a kitchenette, and might include a full kitchen. Bathrooms are usually shower-only for safety reasons.

Many communities have office space for home health services, beauty services, and some have libraries, fitness rooms, media rooms, and game rooms.

Independent living usually has community buses and will arrange transportation to appointments, or shopping, but that's where the inclusive rent fees end.

If your LO can still care for themselves and keep up with their own medicines, it's a great option. And, if your LO needs a little help, you can hire assistants to give them a boost.

- What you pay for: Your apartment and restaurant-style meals in the community dining room. Activities in-house, and some outings. Transportation to some appointments and shopping.
- What's extra: Concierge services (laundry/housekeeping)
- What you don't get: Medical care, Medicine maintenance

Assisted Living

Assisted living gives you everything you find in independent living with a layer of medical attention. In assisted living, your LO can rely on med-techs to dispense their medicine to them, and take that worry from their shoulders. Housekeeping and laundry are alsoincluded in monthly fees.

In assisted living you can expect someone to help your LO with basic hygiene, and help them dress and groom themselves if needed. They may also assist your LO in getting to and from meals, making sure they are eating.

These places are staffed 24/7 so that if your LO needs help, it is available to them, and they all have an RN on staff during business hours.

Pricing is different for all of these communities and is something you'll want to be sure you understand going in. Some communities are all-inclusive, and regardless of your LO's level of need, you pay one price. Others have stepped rates depending on the level of care needed. Usually, your LO will need the community RN to approve them for residence.

If your LO needs some assistance with daily tasks or forgets when it's time to take their medicine, or sometimes needs to be reminded to eat, maybe this is right for you. But bear in mind that the level of independence and autonomy decreases as the levels of care increase. Most assisted living apartments are bare-bones without a kitchenette because stoves are fire hazards.

- What you pay for: Your apartment and restaurant-style meals in the community dining room. Laundry and housekeeping. Medicine routines. Help with hygiene, dressing, and grooming. Activities in-house, and some outings. Transportation to some appointments and shopping.
- What's extra: Depending upon the community, maybe nothing, or maybe the personal services.
- What you don't get: As much autonomy, or a kitchenette.

Memory Care

Gentle Reader, if you're looking into memory care, let me give you a little hug. Because if you even have to think about memory care for a Loved One, you probably need one.

Memory care gives you everything you get in assisted living with the understanding that your LO might think it is 1952 and they are living in a dumpster behind the Don Juan Taco Stand in Grand Prairie, Texas. Or, they might be non-verbal. Or, they might just want to sleep all day. Or they might be escape artists trying to find an open exit so they can make their way back to their platoon.

Memory care can be a sad, scary place, or it can be a wacky, wonderful place based on the staff.

Memory care is not rehab. The staff isn't trained to rehab people's brains (my mother and I have this discussion weekly when she complains they aren't doing enough to make her smart again). But, memory care staff should be working with your LO to keep them engaged.

I'm going to draw a comparison between memory care and the infant or year-old rooms in daycare. What you care most about is how the staff loves on your baby, keeps them clean and fed, warm and safe. You're not so much worried about them learning new tricks, but about them feeling comfortable in their environment, being healthy, fed, and loved.

Like assisted living, some memory care facilities are all-inclusive, and some have stepped rates. Make sure you understand how you will be charged before going in.

If your LO doesn't remember how to take care of themselves or to eat, or how to dress and groom themselves, or if they have an advanced form of dementia, memory care is probably right.

- What you pay for: Your apartment and restaurant-style meals in the community dining room. Laundry and housekeeping. Medicine routines. Help with hygiene, dressing, and grooming. Activities in-house. Transportation to some appointments with an attendant. Extra security and different training for the staff to work with people whose memories are diminished.
- What's extra: Depending upon the community, maybe nothing, or maybe the personal services.
- What you don't get: Independence or the ability to roam freely.

Transitional Communities

Some communities have a mix of independent, assisted, and memory care units. These are fantastic if you think your LO will need to move from one level of care to another because it's usually much easier to move within the community than to have to move to an entirely different property. Sometimes, the community mainte- nance team will even do your move for you.

Nursing Homes

Nursing homes are generally meant for rehab or hospice and aren't really places where people go to live unless they have a need for round-the-clock medical staff. Generally, insurance will cover the cost. Think of nursing homes as long-term hospitals once the patient is in recovery. I'll be honest: They are pretty grim.

Room Type and Roommates

In most communities, you will be offered the choice of having your Loved One live on their own, or with a roommate. The obvious pro to having a roommate is that your LO's rent decreases by as much as $1000 per month. The obvious con to having a roommate is that your LO has dementia, and is no longer a reasonable human being. Usually, if you have a married couple living together in a unit, you are charged one full rate, with one add-on rate to cover food and care level costs. If you have two unrelated people living together in a unit, both of them pay a separate (and hopefully) equal rate and any additional care-related costs per individual.

When my mom moved into independent living, she was in an apartment-style home with a kitchenette, and she lived alone. That worked out really well for her and made her transition from her house into an apartment a little easier.

When I moved her into assisted living, she had a smaller, studio-sized apartment to herself. This also worked well for where both she and her finances were situated. When she was promoted to memory care, we couldn't afford a private room any longer and moved her into a shared suite. At first that was fine because Mom was alone in the suite, but she became very confused when a roommate was added to the room.

I pause here to make an observation: When I talked to my mom, she told me all the horrible things she imagined her roommate was doing, and all the fights they got into, and how much she hated the woman. When I would sneak in to observe her without her seeing me, she was doting on her roommate like she was a younger sibling. The nurses told me how much Mom and her roommate loved each other, and how they went everywhere together. My mom's room-mate told me how much she adored Mom, and Mom would agree, rolling her eyes behind the roommate's back and mouthing, "Blah blah blah."

I think Mom was only telling me the awful things, and telling me what she imagined was happening. I don't think any of the bad things she told me were actually happening.

My son started in daycare when he was five weeks old because I had to go back to work. He did really well up until he was three years old, at which point I had to scrape him from my body to get out of the classroom in the mornings. He would run to the front window that I had to pass to get back to my car, flatten himself against the glass and scream, "Why are you doing this to me?!"

Fifteen minutes later, when I got to work and could turn on the daycare webcam, I would see him playing happily, eating pancakes, drawing, building with blocks, or just dancing by himself to the music they played. He was absolutely fine throughout the day, engaging and laughing. When I picked him up at the end of the day, as soon as he saw me he would start to wail like they'd beaten him for nine straight hours.

I came to think of it like my job. Did I enjoy going to work? Not really. Was I miserable at work? Not really, but I'd rather have been somewhere else. My days weren't generally bad, and I enjoyed a lot of my coworkers and some of my work, so if you'd watched me via webcam, you'd have seen a pretty happy person. But at five o'clock, I was ready to jet! And if you'd told me I needed to stay until seven, I'd have been very sad. That helped me understand him more and be more empathetic.

Taking Away the Keys

He didn't hate where he was and he wasn't being abused or neglected, he would simply rather have been with me. In my absence, he could push that desire aside and make the best of it, just like I did every time I dropped him off, but as soon as he saw me all the emotions he had shoved down in order to survive the day came rushing out of him.

I believe my mom has the same kind of experience in community living, only she never gets to leave. She's always looking for me to come take her home, but home doesn't exist any longer as she would define it. When I come to visit or to take her for outings, she never gets the relief of knowing she gets to go home with me. It's really sad and I struggle with feelings of guilt about that, but just like I had to send my son to daycare because I couldn't afford to stay home, so I found him the best places I could and I made sure he wasn't being abused or neglected, I remind myself that I can't afford to keep my mom in my home, so I have made sure she's in the best place possible.

When she tells me horrible things, I take them with a grain of salt. I take her old advice, "Never believe anything you hear, and only half of what you see." She would be so angry if she knew I said that.

Community sales people will tell you that they will carefully consider your LO's personality and needs when they match them up with a roommate. That has not been our experience. Our experience has been that a roommate match is based on which suites have an empty and available space. So, apply that grain of salt to whatever a sales person tells you.

Between March 2020 and March 2021, my mom had six different roommates. Two of them died from COVID complications, one at the height of the lockdown and one as the world was opening back up again. One moved away. We moved away from a community to get away from one, and then had the same problem with another at a different community, but that community honored their word and fixed the situation.

Mom has seen a lot of death since moving into community living, and that's an added factor in risk to her emotional well-being.

I'd be remiss not to mention that. Having two roommates disappear in ambulances, never to return hit her hard and confused her a great deal. She doesn't remember them now, but she was distraught when it happened.

If your LO has a roommate and there is a problem, discuss that with both their lead nurse and the director of the community, and give them time to address the issue. If your LO has a roommate and your LO is the problem, please work with the community team to get your LO straightened out.

Bad Behavior in Communities

Remember that kid in elementary school who would trip you as you walked past his desk? Or that kid who always whispered behind your back and tried to start rumors? Actually, think about all the kids you went to school with. All those kids are going to get old, some of them will end up with dementia, and some of them will end up living in senior communities. That means, the tripper, the gossiper, the grabber, the bully, the crier–those people all have the possibility of ending up living with (or being) your Loved One in a community.

To me, the only thing worse than finding out your Loved One has been on the receiving end of hurt is finding out that your Loved One is inflicting the hurt.

If your LO is being hurt, you can talk to the staff or even file a complaint with the State Ombudsman. If your LO is being hurtful, you need to have plan that includes doctors, medications, and possibly a different living arrangement.

My mom is kind of a bully and has gotten in trouble in one community for whacking a man with a pool noodle repeatedly (she had a crush on him and that's how she was flirting), jabbing people with knitting needles (she was bored and wanted to liven up the place), smacking people on the back of the head (she didn't think they were alert enough and wanted them to pay attention), andmaking people cry by mocking them. She has also been a huge benefit in a different community because she saw all the residents asher little chicks and she mother-henned them, making things easier for the staff, and making the residents feel loved (or smothered, whoknows?)

I moved her out of the community where she was being anuisance and her behavior changed, making me think her aggres- sion was an offshoot of how she felt about the environment. Ihaven't seen her hit anyone since we moved her away from that community, and she hasn't told me she was going to "beat the shit out of" anyone since she's been in her most recent place.

Remember that paranoia often accompanies dementia, and with paranoia comes fear, and aggression is fear's good friend. If your LO doesn't feel safe, they may not be able to communicate that to you, but their actions will tell you something is wrong. It may take you a while to figure it out what is wrong–that's okay. Do what you can to ensure your LO's safety and do your part to make sure your LO isn't a hazard to the people around them.

How Do I Choose Between My Home and A Home?

So, this is deeply personal. No one can tell you what is right for your family, but you.

I will tell you that my mom and I cared for my grandparents in our home for five years. My grandfather was wheelchair-bound and rarely verbal, with terrible Sundowner Syndrome when they moved in with us. We cared for him through him being bed-ridden with a feeding tube for the last year of his life.

My grandfather's world was the four walls of the living room or the bedroom. I did put some glow-in-the-dark stars on the ceiling for him, and I bought him a goldfish to watch, but that man was miserable and it breaks my heart to think about it.

During the day, while my mom and I worked, we had a sitter come in to keep my grandmother company, and care for my grandfather. My grandmother was bored and angry, and she took out her anger on us in really strange, and sometimes awful ways.

Our house was not built to accommodate their needs, and as we deconstructed it bit by bit to make it work, we destroyed our own property value. The proceeds from the sale of that house became my mother's life savings, so we were literally taking years off how we could accommodate her lifestyle.

Where my grandparents could have been in more comfortable quarters built to accommodate their needs, with medical staff on hand to help with the hardest parts of my grandfather's care, where they could have had diverse company and better meals, and where they could have felt less like obligations and more like residents, I feel like we did them a disservice because my mom had promised to never put them in a home. I deeply regret not pushing my mom and her extended family harder to get my grandparents into proper care.

You may be well-equipped to care for your Loved One in your home.

I am not. I could no more care for my mom than I could fly to the moon. I work full time, have a teenager, am going through menopause, and am the world's worst nurse in the first place. But, with my mom living in memory care, I can be an adoring daughter with the energy to take her out, love on her, and make her feel like a princess.

Okay, But How Am I Supposed To Pay For This?

Friend, I do not know. It's expensive. I am genuinely worried about the Death Math of my mother's finances and what that means for my life when…

While I was writing this book, my dad died. That means greater than two-thirds of my mother's income just stopped suddenly because her spousal support based on his retirement pay stopped.

Weeks prior to his death, he updated his will (as was his right), and any inheritance he had put aside for me moved into a trust to be dispersed after his wife passes. (Which I hope is not for a very long time. She's a lovely woman.) My dad had told me multiple times that he had money set aside and my plan was to take that money and put it into my mom's care. Well, I have to make a new plan. New plan is to win the lottery.

Independent, assisted, and memory care living are incredibly expensive.

For us, we have my mom's retirement pay and her social security, and that covers a third of her rent. We take a little out of her savings every month to cover the rest. When her savings is gone, I will be paying for the rest out of my pocket, unless Medicaid will cover the cost. Maybe I'll sell enough books to cover the cost? Please buy this book for a friend. It makes a great gift.

If you are far enough ahead of planning, you can purchase long-term care insurance. If it's coming right up on you, then it's going to be a matter of what you can afford. And if you can't afford the level of care in a community, you may look into home health- care so that you have trained professionals who can come in and help you with your LO's physical needs.

Your LO might qualify for supplemental social security benefits to help cover the cost of care. Medicaid may cover the cost of some care.

The support groups I frequent regularly suggest to people that they talk to an attorney who specializes in elder law. You can also learn a lot from government websites, but I'll be honest with you: I do not have time for that right now. Although, I guess I could be sitting on hold with Social Security while I write this.

Okay, But How Do I Talk My LO Into Moving?

Every situation is different and complex. I tried to get my mom to consider independent living for five years and she was furious every time I brought it up. Ultimately, she had a health crisis and came to stay at my house for a weekend, and I never took her back to the house she had lived in alone.

Since I'd brought her to my house in my car, she didn't have her car available to her. She was just stuck. When I moved her into her new apartment, I gave her back her car keys, but the Jeep was still sitting in her driveway thirty minutes away, so she couldn't get to it to drive away from the awful (in her mind) prison I'd taken her to. I don't recommend these guerilla tactics for every situation, but in our case, it saved my mom's life, and probably the lives of many other people, given her decline.

The health crisis shocked her into understanding she needed help, so I just moved very quickly and got her into the community I had toured prior to her health event. I was able to hire movers to gether big-ticket items (bedroom and living room) moved into the community within three days, and had her up and running in a week. The move from that apartment in independent living into assisted living was precipitated by another health crisis, and I made that decision and made a full move while she was in the hospital recovering from a stroke.

Similarly, I moved her from assisted living into memory care while she was in a nursing home, rehabbing from surgery. Well, that's the short version of that story, but the point is, I made the decisions and I made the moves, and when she got angry, I just let her be mad. I'd have been mad, too.

Hopefully, this is something you and your LO have agreed upon far in advance, and maybe you've got a list made. Maybe you and your LO have decided that when these 5 things are happening, you both agree it's time to move into a more care-centric community.

Hopefully, you and your LO have already talked with their physician about a long-term plan. It's always best to get a doctor's advice.

If that's not the case and you're making decisions during a crisis, you're just going to have to hold your nose, make the decision, and deal with the consequences. If you have the proper POAs and the car keys, you've got what you need to move your Loved One. They may be very angry with you for a very long time. That's okay.

A Momversation

Ring Ring
    Me: Hello?
    Mom: LANE! Thank God!
    Me: What's wrong?!
    Mom: Lane, I can't find my phone *sobbing** I have lost my phone!
    Me: Mom...Mom...Mom...listen to me. Stop crying. Listen.
    Mom: **snuffle** Okay.
    Me: Mom, you are on your phone. You are using your phone to call me.
    Mom: ...
    Me: Mom? Are you there?
    Mom: I am using my phone to call you?
    Me: Yes. You are calling me from your phone.
    Mom: I am using my phone to call you. Oh my lord. I'm nuts.
    Me: No, you aren't nuts. You're just confused. Like maybe forgetting your glasses are on top of your head, and looking for them everywhere. I've done that. You're okay.
    Mom: Okay.
    Two minutes later
    Ring Ring

Me: Hello?
Mom: Oh, thank god! Lane! I can't find your phone number!

Okay, But How Do I Really Know For Sure It's Time?

For me, I knew my mom couldn't live on her own anymore when I found her wandering around her house pantsless, with no concept of day or time, confused about how to answer the phone and the front door. Her bare backside was a pretty clear signal of distress.

In hindsight, she'd stopped cooking for herself and was buying all her meals from fast food places. I thought she was just tired of cooking or being weird, but she'd lost the executive function to collect food, prepare it into ingredients, and cook a meal. She had stopped answering her phone for days at a time, which I thought was just her being sulky, but was actually that she'd forgotten how to answer her phone and was afraid to ask for help.

I also got a call from the branch manager of her bank, letting me know that she'd lost an unusual number of debit cards and was coming into the branch regularly behaving erratically just days before the pantsless escapade. That was pretty unusual, but I knew the branch manager from when I had worked for that bank, and he looked out for my mom for me.

I'm sure I missed a lot of signals. Here is a list of what you can look for:

- Memory loss
- Difficulty concentrating
- Difficulty carrying out familiar daily tasks
- Struggling with engaged communication
- Being confused about time or place
- Mood changes
- A change in the condition of the home
- Trouble with or anxiety caused by driving
- Unexplained weight loss or weight gain
- Neglecting hygiene, or changes in personal upkeep
- Confusion, frustration, or anger over finances
- Changes in communication

If you see those signs in multiples, you need some help.

Of course, if you can, go to see a doctor with your Loved One and be prepared to be really blunt about what you have observed.

Honestly, that was one of the hardest hurdles for me to overcome: Learning to say in front of my mother, "No, my mother's memory of that is not accurate. What is happening is this." Or, describing my mother's erratic behavior to a doctor in her presence. I started sending emails to clinicians in advance, telling them what to expect and why. That made some things easier.

Actually Taking Away the Keys

My grandmother drove until she felt unsafe behind the wheel, macular degeneration taking her vision, and she gave up her keys gracefully. She did not give up her car gracefully.

She liked to sit outside in the driveway and run the engine and listen to the radio, and she hated for other people to drive her car. A broken hip precipitated a hospital stay, and my cousin was using her car while Grandma convalesced. Ultimately, she died on the operating table as surgeons tried to repair her hip, and in the same hour her car broke down in a spectacular way as my cousin was driving.

Aside from trying to take it with her, my grandmother was a best case scenario: Someone who understood she was no longer able to safely operate a vehicle, who told her family she needed to stop driving.

A few years before they moved in with us, my grandfather caused a very bad car accident. His reflexes gave out on him and he t-boned a young man at an intersection. Though everyone walked away from the accident, my grandfather was so shaken that he told my grandmother he wouldn't be driving anymore. He was afraid he was going to hurt someone else.

My grandfather is the second best case scenario, when someone recognizes they are no longer able to drive and surrenders their keys accordingly, after causing an accident.

To this day, my mother will tell you she's able to drive and she is still extremely salty that I took away her keys.

As I've said, because of Mom's addled state, I was able to get her moved into a safe place, far away from her car before she could argue with me about it. We never had to have the discussion of, "Mom, I think it's time you stop driving," because I took away her choice. If I had given her a choice or a chance to defy logic, I wouldstill be trying to get those keys.

I had stopped letting my son get into the car with her about a year prior to her breakdown. Her friends had started calling me to report that she was driving erratically about six months prior. When I tried to talk to her about it, she shrieked at me and became soangry with her friends for "ratting" her out, she cut off communica- tion with them. I knew the day was coming that I would have totake the keys, but I had no idea how to go about it.

We got lucky that she didn't have an accident. The last time I rode in the car as her passenger, we had a huge fight before she left my house. She had terrified me with her driving because she hadrun red lights, ignored stop signs, and was getting so excited about her conversation with me, that I had to keep yelling, "Watch the road!" She kept turning to make eye contact with me like we were sitting at a restaurant, not flying down the highway.

In hindsight, I should have pushed her harder to give up the keys, or pushed her harder to see a doctor who would have helped diagnose her issues earlier, but I didn't.

I hate confrontation, so even after I had tricked my mother out of her car, I let her keep a set of the keys. Since she had the keys, she had some hope that I might bring her car over to her. I avoided talking to her about it and tried to redirect conversation when she would start asking me to go get her car. When she would ask when Iwas going to give back her Jeep, I would tell her that the doctor had to say she was clear to drive.

Of course, I called the doctor in advance and told him she absolutely should not be on the road, so when she asked him if she could drive, he told her he thought she needed more time and physical therapy to recover her reflexes.

Confrontation aside, it's complicated. I know how much my mom loved to be in her car. I know how my mom associated happi- ness and freedom with the ability to hop in her Jeep and drive for hours. I know how much my mother loved to floor the gas pedal and feel her jowls fly back as she did her absolute best to break the sound barrier in an MG. I knew that taking away my mother's keys was depriving her of one of her greatest pleasures in life, and that broke my heart.

What dementia hasn't taken away from my mother, I have. I have taken away her house, her high heels, three-quarters of her wardrobe, all of her household items save for her bedroom suite, and even then I had to trade out her bed for something smaller, but worst of all, I have taken away her freedom to drive. She says regu- larly, "If I could just get out and drive, I could stand it all."

I have not enjoyed stripping my mother down to a small child's level of autonomy. We have both been embarrassed by it. Mom because she hates to be needy, me because I understand what the loss of dignity is doing to her. There is no easy way to watch your mother pee her pants. There is no easy way to tell your mom she's never going to get behind the wheel again.

While she does still argue with me about it, I think I've been very fortunate because my mom trusts me. As out of it as she has ever been, I have been able to get her to look me in the eye and recognize that I am here to help her, even if the help feels awful.

I tell her, "My job is to keep you safe and healthy. If I can make you happy at the same time, that's great, but my job isn't to make you happy. My job is to keep you alive and well." I've told her that I can and will handle everything but her emotions. I can't do the feeling or the healing for her. I will do everything I am able to do, and I will do it to the best of my ability. Sometimes she won't agree with my choices, and sometimes she might not be happy with my choices, and that's okay. I'm doing my best. My best is never going to be enough for either of us to be perfectly satisfied, but it's all we've got and that's that.

How To Choose Where They Live

Take a Tour

When I found out I was pregnant, almost before the ink on the first sonogram was dry, I was touring daycares. If I was going to have to leave my baby with strangers (and I was), I was going to visit every stranger within range and get on every waiting list, so I increased my chances of choosing the right strangers.

I had put deposits down on three daycares by the time my son was born, and good thing I had because the first day I dropped my baby off at daycare, my mother walked into the center an hour after me and took him out. She told me she had walked in, pointed into his crib and said, "I'm taking that one," and they didn't even put up a fight. I had not put my mother on a list of people allowed to take my baby offsite. Bad security. I moved him immediately.

Moving my mom into independent living was a no-brainer because the community was within walking distance of my house, was nice and clean, and the residents seemed pretty happy. I had toured three places just because I felt like my mom was getting close to needing care, but I wasn't pressed.

When I started looking for assisted living, the heat was a little higher. I used aplaceformom.com to get a list of communities that were within our price and distance range, and I started scheduling visits. When I had narrowed my list down to three, I took Mom to see those places one weekend at a time.

After the last community visit, I took my mom back to her apartment where she promptly had a stroke, and went into the hospital, meaning we were no longer just window-shopping, but we had to find a community post-haste.

When we were looking semi-casually, after confirming affordability, my screening criteria looked like this:

1. Clean
2. Not shabby
3. Residents are clean and their upkeep is good
4. Does not smell like canned green beans and diapers
5. Staff are clean
6. Staff seem happy, or at least do not seem like they are miserable

If they passed my sniff test, we got to my mom's wish list:

1. Church onsite
2. Won't make her play bingo
3. Some kind of physical activities schedule
4. No smoking
5. Good food (we asked to tour during lunch so she could sample)

Those are all things you can observe, or intuit. It's also really important to go in armed with very specific questions, a way to take notes about the answers, and probably some tissues.

Questions to Ask

Before I dive in here, please know that it's okay to cry on these tours. If you're looking for a home for a Loved One, it's probably not because everything is super fine in your world. Your world and your heart are probably a little tender.

I went to one scheduled appointment for a tour and the salesperson wasn't there to show me around and I burst into tears because everything was so hard, and it had been so much effort to schedule the tours and make time for the tours in the first place. I just stood there in that lobby and sobbed. Then, I went out to mycar and I cried some more.

I cried because I was tired. I cried because my mom was sick. I cried because I knew I was going to have to reschedule that tour because that was one of the only places within our budget, and that meant another half day lost to the halls of an old folks home, and I cried because I was embarrassed about crying. When I was finished, I made a note in my notebook that the girl at the front desk had been so kind to me. Then I cried just a little more because some- times kindness makes it worse.

Whenever I went on a tour, I went in with tissues and two lists: My questions and things they needed to know about my mother so they understood my questions.

Things they needed to know about my mom:
- She will try to escape
- She has had colon cancer and has had 3/4s of her colon removed, so she has loose bowels regularly
- She hates BINGO
- She is very paranoid because of past mistreatment
- She loves church
- She needs a walker, but still sometimes trips over her own feet
- She can still "do" for herself, but she needs reminders about hygiene
- She wears adult diapers and uses medicated wipes
- She gets "helping" confused with "hurting" sometimes

How I turned those into questions for each community:
- How do you plan for and prevent elopement? What are

your policies and processes when elopement happens?
- Do you have easily accessible toilets in common spaces? How often do you do laundry? How quickly can someone help my mom clean up if she has an accident?
- What activities do you have and how do you invite people to engage in them?
- How you manage it when your residents are angry or having a bad day?
- How do you respond when a resident makes an accusation of theft?
- What kinds of religious services are available? Do you have any churches that make visitations?
- What steps do you take when a resident falls? How quickly do you notify me? What's the process if someone gets sick and needs care?
- Are your charges all-inclusive, or do you have a step-rate? What are your levels of care? How do you determine if someone needs more care?
- What toiletries do you provide? Do you keep track of supply levels for the residents? How do you alert the family when a resident is running low on supplies? Do you accept subscription deliveries from places like Amazon?
- What do you do when residents become violent or aggressive?

Along with all that, I was armed with reviews from various sources and I would ask them questions specific to the reviews. For example, if they got a one star review from a family that said their communication was terrible, I would ask, "I saw on Yelp that six months ago the Duncan family said they had a lot of issues with communica- tion. Can you tell me how you addressed those concerns?"

Ask anything you want! If you see something while you're walking down the halls, ask about it. I started talking to staff who weren't expecting it (within reason--I wasn't disruptive) just to get a feel for how they might talk to my mom. I tried to keep in mind that how they treated me on the tour, as a prospect, was the best treatment we would ever get.

Paperwork

Prepare for a lot of it. Forms you might need to fill out include:

- Lease agreement
- Medical history
- HIPAA release
- Living Will release (this is a Do Not Resuscitate order)
- Personal profile (likes/dislikes, bullet points of life history)
- Personal items release (against theft, breakage, etc)
- Permission forms (to ride in community vehicles, use community fitness center)
- Medical permission forms (for access to visiting podiatrists/optometrists)

I've even had to sign a release stating that my mother will not run over anyone with her walker, a wheelchair, or an electric scooter! I really wanted to sign that one, "No promises."

It can take between forty-five minutes and two hours to finalize a lease agreement with a community, so be prepared and take snacks. I never take my mom with me when I'm finalizing a lease because the process takes so long and it reminds her of how much she can't do for herself. I did make the mistake of taking my teenager once. He hasn't forgiven me, yet.

You will need to have a few things with you when you sign a

lease. If your Loved One can sign for themselves, you won't need to show your ID, but if you plan to sign for your Loved One, you will need the following:

- Your ID and your Loved One's ID
- Your Power of Attorney, showing that you have the right to sign for your Loved One
- Your banking information if the community requires a direct deposit for payment
- Your Loved One's insurance information, medical history, and a list of current medications

Be ready to write checks for a community fee (which is basically your security deposit, but you will not get any of it back), and your first month of rent. As soon as you have the executed lease agreement, you need to immediately purchase renter's insurance to make sure your Loved One's things are covered in case of damage.

Pro Tip: Don't put anything valuable or priceless in your LO's apartment, especially in memory care. Residents get lost and go into other people's apartments all the time, and sometimes they pick up objects that catch their eye. My mom went into a community with one remote control for her TV. She left with five. (She also knocked over another resident's TV and we were on the hook to buy him a new one. And, another resident got lost, thought my mother's rocking chair was a toilet, pooped on it, then carried the fecesaround the apartment smearing it on everything she could find. Shit literally happened.)

The Actual Work of Moving

I make no bones about the fact that I threw a lot of money at my mother's problems to make them go away. Moving her out of her home and into a senior community is where the biggest chunk of that money went.

My mom had been in her house for thirty-five years when I moved her into independent living. My grandparents had also moved their life into her house for more than five years. When it was time to move my mom, I was looking at the accumulation of more than seventy years of life. I was also looking into a vacuum of despair because my mom had begun hoarding and I couldn't even find a pathway through. I had to excavate a path for myself.

Because my mom's move was sudden, I kept her in my home until I could get her into the senior community. When we finalized her lease, I hired movers to take the big pieces of furniture that I knew she would need, and I packed enough clothes for a few weeks, her towels and linens, some kitchenware, and toiletries and moved those myself.

Honestly, I should have stopped there.

When you move your LO, you may be tempted to fill their new home with as much of their old home as possible. Don't do that.

Ultimately, that leads to more confusion for them and more work for you. Your LO needs a comfortable bedroom and a nice place to sit, but most of their time (especially in memory care) will be spent in the communal spaces, so you don't need to kill yourself to outfit them in splendor.

Once my mom was in her community home, I spent the next six weeks going to her house after work and on weekends, trying to get it cleaned out to the point that I could a.) figure out what needed to be in her new apartment with her, b.) get it ready to sell.

At week seven, I was working in the living room when a man just walked right into the house. He had seen that I was working on it and wanted to know if I was selling it. He started pressuring me topromise to sell it to him. I was terrified! I got him out of the house and locked the front door.

A little while later, as I was hauling bags of trash to the curb, a different man walked in the front door while my back was turned. I went back into the house to find him checking out the den. He was another "potential buyer" who wanted to give me his information so I could sell to him first.

While I was happy knowing that I could probably sell the place, I was really freaked out by the people who just helped themselves to the front door. That was the final straw for me. I rented a dumpster. I hired a service that specialized in clearing out hoarder nests. I stopped going over to the house alone.

It took the service a week to clear out the house, but when they had finished, I had neat stacks of important paperwork they had found, jewelry my mother had lost, and $700 in coin they had gathered. I also still had my sanity and no one had murdered me.Solid win!

Do It Yourself

You can do it yourself. It will be a lot more cost effective to do it yourself, but it might be more expensive emotionally. Obviously, I don't know your situation. I just want to be sure you know that just because you can, doesn't mean you have to. We've all moved before.

Taking Away the Keys

We all know what a huge undertaking it can be. Moving your mom out of her house is that undertaking multiplied by the emotional burden. Be sure you're going to have enough energy left over from the move to deal with how your Loved One reacts to it because they will definitely have an emotional response to the move that will require your physical presence and mental sharpness.

Things you'll need/need to know:

- Days/Hours during which the community allows movers
- Will you have access to a freight elevator
- Is there onsite maintenance to help set up furniture/television/cable
- Any restrictions on hanging items
- DEFINITELY get straps to anchor bookshelves or taller furniture to the wall
- If the community has any volume restrictions—as in, closet volume. Some memory cares will ask you to limit the amount of clothing you bring in for your LO.

Hiring Specialists

I do highly recommend finding a senior move specialist if you choose to hire someone. It is likely that your LO's new community will have recommendations from other residents or residents' fami-lies. If you are in North Texas, I recommend Settle In Solutions, and I give their card to every community I visit to share with fami-lies. A specialist will take some photos of the home your LO is leav-ing, and will work with those to decorate their new space to be the tiny house version of what they are used to.

I've moved my mom three times since that first major move. Each time, I've had Settle In Solutions come help her. They start in the early morning, and my mom has a beautiful, serene new spaceby early afternoon.

Bonus, if you hire a specialist, they will take care of gathering all the bullet points above.

Health Care

Urinary Tract Infections

Before I go a step further, I need to remember to tell you about Urinary Tract Infections (UTIs), those pesky devils that turn the sweetest angel into a Tasmanian devil.

Healthline.com says, "The classic symptoms of a urinary tract infection (UTI) are burning pain and frequent urination. UTIs may not cause these classic symptoms in older adults. Instead, older adults, especially those with dementia, may experience behavioral symptoms such as confusion."

Confusion is a gross understatement. An elderly person might only be confused, but they also might become absolutely psychotic. If you see an overnight change in your Loved One, especially if your LO wears adult diapers, get them checked for a UTI posthaste. To make this even worse, somehow, dementia is a possible factor in causing a UTI.

My mom gets them so frequently that I can spot the symptoms and usually get her doctor to prescribe antibiotics swiftly. For her, UTIs bring out the absolute worst of her nightmarish fears and trigger her most truculent behavior. Regardless, whenever she has a

UTI, she ends up telling me that she is somehow living in a railroad boxcar. If she starts talking about trains, I start asking for antibiotics.

Doctors You Need

If you suspect your Loved One is showing signs of dementia, the best place to start is going to be your General Practitioner/Family Doctor. That doctor will be able to refer you to specialists like neurologists, psychiatrists, and geriatric specialists. Each of those doctors will probably do an intake interview that includes some cognitive testing, but each one will also access different types of labsto help narrow down the diagnosis.

When I got my mom started seeing a GP, after four visits in two months, with careful review of her medical history, a lot of questions for both her and for me, he wrote the diagnosis of vascular dementia. He felt there was adequate evidence that her muddled state was caused by a combination of high blood pressure from a decade of untreated heart disease, and high blood sugar from atleast a decade of untreated diabetes. She had also had a TIA and undergone open heart surgery, had a few concussions, and wasgenerally not taking great care of her health.

When she had a stroke, she had an MRI in the emergencyroom. The attending physician there showed me where the stroke had affected the executive function center of her brain, and told me that if she had Alzheimer's we'd be seeing—honestly, I don't remember. I'd been awake for thirty-two hours at that point and I'm not even going to pretend I understood what he was telling me or that I remember his exact words.

The bottom line was that he didn't think she had Alzheimer's, and he stressed to me that while her vision might improve (the stroke caused partial, temporary blindness), her executive function would not. The circuit board was fried.

Out of the hospital, we saw two neurologists. Each got copies of her labs. The first one had a short conversation with her, and when she asked if she could drive, said, "I don't see that there is anything wrong with you. I think you're fine to drive."

I sat there horrified, knowing my mother had forgotten how to open a door and was stuck on her third floor balcony for two hours before anyone at her independent living community figured out she was waving for help, not being friendly. I mentioned that to the doctor and he said, "Normal memory loss."

And I said, "Thank you." And decided to get a second opinion.

My mother was gleeful as we drove away. "He said I was normal," she crowed. "Now you can give me back my car."

That's when I had to remind her that we had sold her car. In fact, it had been her idea to sell the car. After a short snit, she crossed her arms and said, "Then I'll just get a job and buy a new one."

The second neurologist, after almost the exact same set of questions to my mother, said, "Mrs. Morris, you definitely show signs of dementia." Then, he explained that he couldn't really provide a diagnosis, but he could rule things out. He could rule out Alzheimer's, he could rule out hydrocephalus, he could rule out Parkinson's or things like that. He went on to explain the tests that would be required to rule out Alzheimer's and I opted out.

With no family history, based on her medical history and her MRI, her GP felt certain she did not have Alzheimer's, and even the second neurologist said he thought it was highly unlikely, but that he couldn't rule it out without doing the tests. He didn't think the tests were necessary for my mom, but it was up to her.

This was one of those value decisions I had to make. If she did have Alzheimer's perhaps there were treatments that could help her, but after the stroke and with her history, the likelihood of reversing any issues were null. My mother's level of fear of MRIs and CT scans was enough for me to say, "Nevermind". We moved onto the psychiatrist.

After a visit with my mom he put her on medication to help with depression and anxiety. It took us several months to find the right fit, but once we did, her life was greatly improved.

Since moving into memory care, Mom has seen a geriatric specialist as her general practitioner. Her doctor makes regular visits to Mom in her home, so she can observe her in familiar, comfort- able surroundings, outside the stress of a doctor's office visit. Working with someone who focuses on senior citizens has been beneficial to us and Mom's physical health has improved exponen- tially since receiving specialized care.

Emergency Room Visits/Hospital Stays

When I was pregnant, I kept a Go Bag in my car. So, if I went into labor, I had everything with me I needed. The one day I didn't have that bag, I went into labor. Of course.

As my mom's Person, I keep a Go Bag ready for when we go visit the ER. Back in 2008, when we were dealing with her cancer, then again in 2014, when we were dealing with her heart I was spending a lot of time in emergency rooms, and hospital waiting rooms. I started packing a bag with necessities and nice-to-haves to get me through the long hours.

Now, I have a little Go Kit instead of a whole bag. I keep it on a shelf in my pantry, so when I'm heading to the ER, I can just grab it on my way out the door. I always take:

- A phone charging cable and wall wart (that little thing you plug into the wall, that you plug your charging cable into—my techie husband swears this is its name)
- An external phone battery (charged up)
- Granola bars
- 2 bottles of water
- Extra socks and a change of underwear

- A small photo album with pictures of my son as a toddler (because it distracts my mom from pain or discomfort, or just soothes her to look at his baby pictures and remember good times.)
- Photocopies of her ID, insurance cards, medication list, and medical history (because in a true emergency, sometimes I don't remember all the details)

This way, when I get a call that my mom has fallen and needs x-rays, I am ready to spend half or all of my night sitting up with her and can answer all the questions every nurse and doctor asks me.

How to Advocate

After a fall, my mom and I spent a few hours in the ER. Her community called an ambulance, and I met her there. Someone missed a note that my mom came from memory care, and theperson who did my mom's intake did so under the impression that she was fully able to advocate for herself.

After they completed a CT scan, the ER doctor came in to talk with her and introduced himself to me. As he walked up to Mom, she asked him who he was, so he laughed and said, "I'm your doctor."

And she said, "Well, you introduced yourself to her..."

And he said, "Oh! You don't remember me!"

And she said, "Did I meet you?"

He looked over at me, and I watched bonhomie slide down his face like Crisco in a hot pan, replaced by confusion, then some horror. "Is this normal?" he asked.

I nodded, "She's in memory care."

His expression settled somewhere around "Oh dang, that could have been bad." and he nodded at her chatter, then he looked back at me and said, "She fakes it really well! I thought—Wow— Okay. That's good to know."

And I did the little speech about vascular dementia and a stroke, and his shoulders went up around his ears.

Taking Away the Keys

He said again, slowly, almost reverently, "She's really good."

I said, nodding my agreement and weary wisdom, "I know."

When he left the room, Mom grinned at me. "He said I faked it really good!" She was so proud. "He thought I was normal! Maybe I'm getting better!"

I'm in several groups with people whose parents have gone round the bend. Every couple of months, a new person posts about a doctor not believing them that their Loved One is completely demented. Every couple of months, we all chime in and tell the distressed newbie that they need a second opinion and not to feel bad—no matter how hard the doctor was on them.

Many people with dementia are able to fake their way through situations like they are perfectly whole, and you only realize there is a problem when it's too late—like the way my mother was adamant with the ER staff (before I arrived) that while she may have been prescribed medication, she certainly never took it.

They had been treating her like she had no medication in her system (which caused a problem but nothing terrible), and couldn't understand why her blood sugar was so good if she was diabetic, but wasn't taking anything. She's THAT convincing.

I second guess myself ALL the time. Sometimes I leave a visit thinking, "Does she really belong in memory care?" Then she'll call me and tell me she's in a boxcar behind Don Juan's in Grand Prairie. Or, we'll be having a conversation and I'll think, "Wow! She really is improving!" And she'll say, "Now, I know Mother and Daddy couldn't get out here, but are you going to go get them?" And I know better.

A home health nurse told me that patients like my mom are fantastic at faking because that's how they cope with stress. She had warned me that I would see a sudden, sharp downturn in her mental acuity once she settled into cared-for-living and her stress levels reduced. She was right!

Anyway, it was just funny and terrifying thinking that the doctor had believed my mom was capable of conducting herself well, and I wonder how many scenarios flashed in front of his eyes as he realized that 90% of everything she'd told him was probably just made up?

To be a good advocate for your Loved One you must:

1. Be Available. First and foremost you have to be present in some way. When my mom was in the hospital and I couldn't be there to talk to her doctors because I was at work, I called frequently and left notes. I also took gifts to the nurses because I knew I was driving them crazy with all my calls.
2. Be Informed. You have to know what your Loved One's diagnosis is, be well-versed in how that diagnosis affects their everyday life, know what medications they are taking (and for what), and have a decent idea of their daily routine.
3. Have no shame. You have to be a gadfly. Hospital negligence nearly killed my mother once, and if I hadn't gone Terms of Endearment in the middle of the hospital floor, they would have let her code. I hate making a scene. I hate disagreeing with authority figures. Still, it's better for me to be embarrassed or look like an asshole, than for my mother to be dead. That's just the bottom line. Ask questions until you are comfortable. Demand the care you think your Loved One needs until you are satisfied. Be polite and respectful, but don't be afraid to stand in the middle of a busy hospital floor and demand help.

How Much Do You Tell Them?

Just as I was putting the finishing touches on the first draft of this book, my mother started acting like she had another UTI. I asked her doctor to check on her, and her doctor asked for permission to do an ultrasound. One thing led to another, and we were booking a CT scan a day after the ultrasound results came back. The day after that, we were booking a surgery, and getting new referrals to oncologists for even more appointments.

I was sharing with friends that I'm really worried because our best case scenario is still at least two more painful procedures away, and worst case means I will have to decide whether to extend my mother's crumbling life with chemotherapy and radiation treatments, or sign up for hospice.

After notifying my boss of the time off I needed for surgery (not much now that I am a remote worker and can take my laptop to the waiting room with me) and potential upcoming appointments, Ispent ten minutes ugly-crying to my husband about wanting to turn back time and somehow trick my parents into having an oldersibling for me—someone else to be in charge.

I do not want to be in charge right now, but someone has to be. For me, being in charge means making all the major medical decisions for my mom as well as deciding how much my mom knows about her own health. There is a lot to consider there. The bottom line is I have to weigh every ounce of information against my mother's mental and emotional well-being. In our case, from experience I know that if I tell my mom her condition, she won't remember exactly what I've said to her, but she will remember that something is wrong. She will fret and worry, and that worry will turninto anxiety and weird, self-harming behavior.

So, I'm not going to tell her what's going on until I show up to take her to the appointment, and even then, she's going to get a simplified version of the truth.

As I keep repeating, every situation is different. I relay the information that my mom is able to understand and process, in a timeframe that works for how she understands and processes.

Dispensing Medication

I employed guerrilla tactics on a lot of things with my mom. In a lot of ways, I feel like I trapped a feral cat and tried to make it an indoor pet. I coaxed her into my car that one time, and I never took her back to her house again. I tricked her into an urgent care, then got her into an ER and established with a physician, and started her on heart and diabetes medication.

My mom was pretty resistant to a medication routine. I was brand new to this caregiving world, and wasn't sure if she didn't want to take the medicine or couldn't. She had two pills to take in the morning, and one at night.

We honestly fought like cats and dogs about it. Finally, after I yelled, "Do you want to die, Old Woman?! Or do you want to live to see your grandson graduate?!" She agreed to get with the program, but then she also admitted she was having trouble remem- bering. Reminders, I could manage.

At first, I called her twice a day to tell her to take her pills, but I had a job and a kid in sports, and I couldn't do that seven days a week, so I set alarms on her phone.

We were working with a standard AM/PM pill case, but instead of taking AM then PM, she would take AM then AM. She couldn't go up and down on the pill case, only in a straight line.

So, I bought two separate pill cases, one for AM, one for PM. You know what happened. It didn't work. I tried three other methods before I gave up and got really basic and found something that worked.

First, I bought an Alzheimer's clock that showed her the Day, the Date, the Time, and the Time of Day. Since she could remember her morning pills, I got ziplock baggies and wrote the days of the week and MORNING on them, to match the Alzheimer's clock. I used velcro strips to stick them to her cabinets, right above her kitchen sink, eye level, where they were highly visible and in a place she went to often. Then I set an alarm on her phone to tell her to go take those pills.

Next, I bought a pill case with an alarm for her night meds, and set that for 8pm because she was usually back in her room from dinner by then. When it was time for her to take those pills, the case would beep and the day of the week section of the case would light up red, so she knew which one to open. The case would alarm until she opened it.

On Sunday nights, I would go over and fill up her baggies and case for the week, and I would go over it with her.

1. Look at your clock
2. Match the day on your clock to the day on your baggie
3. Take those pills
4. Listen for your alarm
5. Look for the red light
6. Take those pills

On Wednesday nights, I would go over and make sure she was on track, switch around any baggies she had mixed up, and go over the routine with her again. Was it ugly looking? Yes. Did it work? Also, yes.

For six glorious months, my mother took her medication with no issue. Then, she had a stroke and a massive regression of executive function and she just couldn't make it happen for herself anymore.

You do have options when it comes to medication. Be sure you talk to your medical team for advice.

- Self-Regulated: Your Loved One is able to understand what to take, when to take it, and has the capacity to do this on their own.
- Assisted: Your Loved One might need reminders to take medication that is laid out for them, but can still understand the how and the why well enough to manage with a little help.
- Provided: Your Loved One is no longer able to fully grasp the how or why of their medication well enough to take it consistently, or possibly doesn't have the capacity to understand timing. In this case, you would want someone to be available to give your Loved One their medication at the same times every day, and confirm that the medication has been taken.

A Momversation

Mom: Did I tell you I talked to a man who teaches Psychology at UT?
Me: No. How neat.
Mom: Yes. He said I was better educated than he was, and that I could do more with patients with just words than he could do with his whole medical practice.
Me: Wow!
Also Me: I need to find out his name and notify the board.
Mom: Yes. He offered me a job. He said he'd like to have me come teach at his school.
Me: And what did you say?
Also Me: This is going to be like the time an occupational therapist said she wanted to work with Mom and what she meant was work with her as a patient and I had to break it to Mom that she didn't have a job offer.
Mom: I told him he had too many women following him around and I wasn't going to get mixed up in an affair with him.
Me: I'm glad to hear that
Also Me: Well, that took an unexpected turn.
Mom: Yes, so he introduced me to his wife. I really want you to meet her. They live here.

Me: Oh! How nice!

Also Me: Oh! He's another inmate!

Mom: Yes. It's very nice. I guess when I get out of here, I can teach mental health.

Me: That sounds like a plan.

The Emotional Side

Doing Your Best

Before I even get started here, I want to define what I mean by "doing your best."

Doing your best is going to look different for every person and every situation. It does not mean pouring 100% of your time and energy into your Loved One.

For me, doing my best looks like making sure my mom is in a secure, peaceful community where she gets the best care we can afford for her. It means keeping up with her doctor's appointments, keeping her toenails clipped, taking her for haircuts, and visiting regularly. That's it. After that, I'm tapped out. I have a whole other person to raise and parent, a job, a husband, friends, and my own life to live.

For a friend of mine, doing her best looks like caring for her father in her home, while she raises her family. She manages every aspect of her father's care as a stay-at-home mom and caregiver. Her best also includes siblings who give her a break every other month, so she can get away and rest.

Our bests look very different, but both of our parents are

equally as well cared for, are equally as healthy, are equally as happy.

Best isn't about the quantity you can give. It's about the quality of the quantity.

My mom gets about 5% of my physical in-person time, but probably 30% of my mental time which includes 15% more physical time in the form of communicating with doctors, therapists, and her community caregivers, doing her taxes, and filling out insurance paperwork. That's not a lot of physical time spent in the same room with her, but it is my best.

Figure out what your best looks like, then do that, or do as close to that as you are able.

A Momversation

I am usually pretty good at holding myself together with my mom. I look for the humor and try really hard to frame every interaction as a scene. It helps me, and it helps her.

One day, she was so much herself that I started to cry because some stuff is going on, and I just wanted my mom. And there was my mom—but I couldn't burden her with the stuff because it would come back to her in the middle of the night as something entirely different and fully nefarious, but it was so unfair to have her sitting right there, looking like my mom, and sounding like my mom.

I completely broke down and cried like a baby, and had to make up something that wouldn't upset her later.

She hugged me and comforted me, and in a way I think it was a gift to her to get to feel like a mother for a minute, instead of feeling like she was my ward. Then, she capered for me like I do for her, to make me laugh and cheer me up.

Before I left, she had completely forgotten what had happened.

I really miss her. I try to keep that pushed way back in the darkest parts of my heart because I can't focus on the grief of such a slow, continual, ceaseless loss. It's overwhelming. When those feelings sneak past the gatekeepers of logic and discipline, whoa. It's hard to get back under control.

There's no right way to live with dementia. There's no right way to love someone with dementia. There's no right way to present yourself and reality to them because you and reality are shifting alongside everything else in their fantastical brains.

I guess the best we can do is just show up and keep showing up, no matter how hard it gets.

(Then, B and I had to take turns with the kid between Urgent Care and the Children's ER with a double ear infection that had him in tears. That was a LONG day.)

Arguing With Dementia

Arguing with Dementia

Regularly, since we started this journey, my mother will tell me she's been in a railroad boxcar. Sometimes, she's in a boxcar behind the Don Juan's taco stand in Grand Prairie, Texas. Sometimes she is in a boxcar that has been dumped under the Bush library at SMU. Sometimes she has been riding in a boxcar that has been dropped out of an airplane. I don't know if she was a hobo in a past life, but there is a definite fixation on boxcars and usually when she mentions one I know she has a UTI.

Recently, I visited and she told me, "I have been sitting with that girl who died of AIDS in a boxcar and we hit a bump and all these boxes exploded open and I said, 'There are all my blue jeans!' And she said, 'And there are all my blue jeans too!' And I said, "Well let's get them before anyone else can!' and we did. And we scrambled up all our blue jeans and that's how I got fourteen pair of blue jeans. But I've only got two pair here and so I know they stole them all."

Bless my heart. I burst out laughing. I told her I was going to go count all the blue jeans in her closet just so I could walk away and not laugh right at her.

Experts tell you not to argue with dementia. They tell you not to correct or remind patients. I'm no expert. My experience is that sometimes, when a Loved One is just confused, reminding and gently correcting is the right thing to do. When a Loved One is deep in a belief, getting into their world with them is the right thing to do.

I can see a difference now between when my mom is confused about something, and when she really believes something. If she really believes something, like that she's been hanging out on a boxcar with a dead woman, I can't argue with her. I just ask her leading questions until we can get out of that room in her brain. (And try not to laugh because her imaginary adventures are funny.)

If she's confused about something like she sometimes forgets she's divorced or that her parents are dead—she knows she is divorced and she knows her parents are dead, but she can't make the connections (it's hard to explain, but I know it when I run into it with her)—then I can help her unravel the knot and she can find her own way out of the room in her brain.

On the day she'd been in a boxcar full of exploding blue jean boxes, I was late getting over to see her and I guess I upset her internal Lane Clock. As I was driving to her, both my uncle and her nurse called me to tell me she was acting nutty. She'd had the care-giver dial my uncle to ask him where their mother was. In the moment, she was so focused on feelings of wanting her mother, she couldn't remember anyone but her brother, and she couldn't communicate that she was missing their mom.

She could only communicate worry that she couldn't get to their mom, and her brain could only translate that out in questions that alarmed him. I had seen this before in person, but that day something clicked. She just wanted her mom, and she wanted to talk to someone whose feelings could match hers, but her brain was only up to translating feelings into words in present tense at an intermediate level.

When I got there, she asked me again about her mother and I explained and she got really upset because she's self-aware enough to know that asking folk about dead people is a surefire way to make those folks believe you have gone around the bend. She doesn't want anyone to think she's "nuts".

When we talked about it, I stumbled across some magic words that lit up her whole face and gave her some relief. Honestly, they gave me some relief, too, because that was when I realized I could see the difference between confusion and belief in her. That helped give me a whole other way to connect with her.

Mom: I called Junebug.

Me: I know. He let me know you were upset.

Mom: I had to have those people call him for me.

Me: And that was smart of you.

Mom: [fear/frustration/anger] I know Mother is dead! I know Mother is buried! I know you aren't my mother.

Me: [patting/hugging] I know.

Mom: Junebug thinks I'm crazy.

Me: No, he doesn't.

Mom: Do you?

Me: No more than you've always been.

Mom: Ha! I know Mother is dead. Just sometimes...

Me: [I let the pause go until she looked distressed] Sometimes you get confused because your brain goes time traveling without you.

Mom: Yes! I get confused. My brain does like to travel.

Me: Makes sense! You like to travel. Now, you don't get out much with your body, so your brain's just booking flights all over the place.

Mom: I like that. My brain is going on trips. You know I'm not crazy?

Me: Yes. I know it's just confusion. There's a difference between confusion and belief.

Mom: Yes!! I don't believe Mother is alive. I just...

Me: You just want to see her so much, the feeling gets so big, it feels like she might be alive and it gets confusing.

Mom: YES!!

Me: I understand. I totally understand.

Mom: Good.

Me: Good.

Mom: (considering/nodding/moving on) Now, what are we going to do about my blue jeans?

A Momversation

My mom called me last night, absolutely losing her mind in rage. When I got her calmed down to just hissing and spitting, she said, "I'm leaving here! I've got a good thumb and a pretty leg, and those will take me places!"

Then, she thought for a second and murmured, "Might not be the kind of places I want to go, though."

Their Emotions

I Want

I was reading in one of the dementia support groups I frequent and someone was asking about how to manage the entitlement that seems to have settled on her loved one as her disease progresses.

I have to tell you, that entitlement is one of the funniest and one of the most frustrating things with my mom.

I look at it like this: When a baby is born, they don't know themselves from their caretakers. They are the ultimate in entitled beings because they can't separate themselves from their needs and they can't separate their needs from the people around them. Everything is interconnected for them. They simply ARE, and that's that. They are tiny balls of WANT.

Toddlers, who are starting to understand that Caregiver is a separate entity, still function at a high entitlement level because as they are growing into Self and learning that interconnection doesn't necessarily mean intertwined, they aren't capable of being fully considerate of others. That's a learned and practiced skill. This is when they start to learn to share, start to learn to care, and start to learn empathy and compassion. We hope.

But, ultimately a toddler's job is to demand. They do it well!

As kids grow, they accumulate a complex system of filters (much like we accumulate stuff), and learn by cause and effect to ask rather than demand. By the time we're adults, many of us are socialized to be embarrassed to ask for things. The more specific the want, the less likely we are to ask for it because of those empathy filters, or guilt filters, or whatever life has beaten into us. We might even be embarrassed to send back a meal at a restaurant when it isn't what we want.

Toddlers? Not so! Even if you give them exactly what they asked for, they exercise the right to change their minds and demand you to change along with them.

Dementia and various brain-altering diseases chip away at all those filters. The brain is like, "Okay, in order to survive, I need this, this, and this. I don't need this," and it Marie Kondos those filters first. Those filters do not bring joy.

My mother's filters are nearly all gone. She will read you to filth without a second thought, and she wants peanut butter, dammit. If you show up without a gift of food, why did you even come?

She knows what she wants and she asks for it. And she asks and asks and asks because there is no filter to tell her, "Hey, you're kind of demanding." And one of the other things her brain kicked out for not sparking joy was embarrassment.

Embarrassment does not add one thing to her life, or make her survival any easier, so her brain has binned it. She is shameless now. Is her skirt tucked into her underwear and you can see half her butt hanging out of the massive wedgie tucked between her cheeks? Fffff. That's your problem. Quit looking if you don't like it.

She does not register that she's a hassle. And she is. She is demanding and though she is vocally appreciative, it is never enough. She is an endless void of WANT.

I know I am watching her brain do a full decluttering of filters and function until all that will be left is how to pump blood through veins and breathe. Eventually, her brain will decide those no longer spark joy, and will do the final deep clean so she can move into a new space.

We are not getting the security deposit back on the old one.

A Momversation

My mom has always been locationally-challenged. That is, she could always get lost in a strip mall. My childhood was basically us getting in a car and getting lost for three hours until she could find someone to give us directions back home. I cannot tell you how much time we spent in malls, trying to find the door we entered through, or the car in the parking lot.

Now, losing mental acuity, she actually gets lost in the wing of a building that is literally a square. Basically, whenever she turns a corner in the square, she goldfishes and thinks she is in a new building.

Lately, Mom thinks she's been moved into different buildings several times a day. That is, she goes down a hall to the end where the dining room is. That's one building. She turns that corner into the activity room, that's a second build- ing. She turns a corner down the hall to the common living room, and that's another building.

It wouldn't be a big deal, but she's really angry about it. I'm still feeling out the best way to respond so that she feels heard and reassured.

I have worked my way down a list from being reasonable and reassuring, to just letting her talk without really responding beyond, "Oh, wow." So far, I haven't hit on the magic combination.

It reminds me of when Thor was an early toddler and he was trying so hard to convey information, but he didn't have the language skills. He would just melt down because he was trying so hard and he couldn't make me understand. He felt helpless and hopeless and all I could do was try to empathize.

One day, he was struggling because he wanted to see the Jarf. He was SURE I knew what the Jarf was. He was SURE! I had seen the Jarf. I knew the Jarf. Why couldn't I just get him the Jarf?!

That baby cried so hard--he was so frustrated! He cried until he gagged himself, then he cried harder because that was so upsetting. He cried until he wore himself out.

I don't know what synapses fired, but all of a sudden (many, many hours later) I realized he was trying to say sheriff. He wanted to watch the movie Cars, to see the Sheriff.

Turns out he was right all along—I did know the Jarf and how to get the Jarf for him, and the whole time I was saying I didn't know/didn't understand, his frustration was valid and real.

I have tried to remember that anytime he's talked to me about anything since, and now I apply it to my mom. I try to find the hidden piece that is the truth behind the frustration. It isn't exactly the same, but it helps me empathize. The problems are very real to her, whether I understand them or not.

Today, when she complained about having to go to a new building, I tried, "Oh! That's nice they are taking you to see new things! What new did you see?" And it shook her brain loose of the fear and anger long enough for her to look at the situation differently.

She answered, "Oh, shoot. I don't know. But I have things TO DO, Lane. I don't have time to be hopping all over town."

And that allowed me to redirect her by asking what she's planning to do, and we avoided another meltdown.

I just have to figure out my mom's Jarf.

I Want To Go Home

Home means something very different when your memory is taking leave. Home isn't necessarily somewhere. It can be someone or some*when*. For my mom, "home" is with her parents in Columbus, Georgia. Unfortunately, her parents are dead, and their house was sold. There is no way home for her.

Sometimes, home is with me. She desperately wants to live with me. I desperately want not to smother her in her sleep, so living with me is not an option.

Teepa Snow, whose teaching I highly recommend, reminds caregivers that sometimes when a Loved One is asking to go home, they are making a request that has nothing to do with a former address. Rather, they may be trying to tell you:

1. They have an unmet need. They may be hungry, or cold. They may be feeling sad, or frustrated.
2. Their environment is making them uncomfortable. It might be physical discomfort. It might be sensory discomfort. They might be feeling paranoid or unsafe.
3. They want to go outside, or change where they are sitting. Sometimes it is as simple as a change of scenery.

4. Something they can't remember how to express.

Our job is to crack the code.

Our other job is to remember what these grown adults have lost, and treat them with empathy.

When my son was little, I used to commiserate with him when he threw a tantrum over something that seemed ridiculous to me. "Poor guy. You live in a world of No, don't you? The answer to every question is no. You can't put that in your mouth. You can't climb up there. You can't ride the dog. You can't play in the street. You can't even always say what you mean. All you wanted was the blue cup and now you can't even have that."

My mom used to be able to eat what she wanted, go where she wanted, see who she wanted, say what she wanted, and communicate her desires very clearly. Now she's stuck in a place where they tell her what she's going to eat, I tell her where she can go, she only sees people who make time to visit with her, and can't even have a dog. That's hard!

I remember how I felt when I was in my teens but couldn't drive yet. I was aching for the freedom that being able to drive would give me. I was craving the ability to determine my own space in time. I remember how it felt to get that driver's license and be able to go wherever I wanted to go. I remember that freedom.

I cannot imagine what it is going to feel like when my son has to take my keys away one day. It's going to be gutting.

I try to keep all of that in mind when I'm dealing with my mom's outbursts.

I Want To Die
I hope you don't experience this level of distress, but based on what I see in the dementia groups I'm in, and based on my own mother, your Loved One may beg to die, or insist that they willharm themselves.

You definitely need someone with specific training to help you through this, so find and speak to an expert.

I'm going to tell you this: I look at my mom's life and I understand why she is sometimes suicidal. She has lost all her freedom

Taking Away the Keys

and every ability to initiate the interactions she loved most. She is well enough to know what's gone, but not well enough to always express that. She is well enough to know she is unwell, but can't remember why. She feels like a burden. She is lonely. She is sad. I hear her, and I understand.

It's really easy for me to stumble over my ego when my mom starts saying these things. I feel like she is casting aspersions on the work I've done to care for her. Recently, when I saw my mom, she was tired and angry, weepy and fussy, and telling me she felt like I had thrown her away and hated her. She said if this was how she had to live, she might as well die.

Those are the hardest conversations for me to have with her because along with the compassion and hurt I feel for her, I'm also battling with my ego. I get angry that she's saying she feels thrown away and wants to die because it feels manipulative, and because I want her to recognize I'm trying hard for her.

She can't recognize that all the time, though. So, I ask her to look around and we talk about the things in her room, and I say things like, "It's okay for you to have the feelings you are having. I also want you to be able to look around and see how much you are loved. I want you to see your pretty room and know that's an expres-sion of my love."

We hold hands and she cries and begs to come live with me, and I explain that I am not able to take care of her (because if I try to ignore it, she gets angry and if I lie and say soon, she tries to pack and is upset for days.) I make her the same promises: my best might not look like her preferences, but it is my best. She is safe and she is cared for, and ultimately I tell her that she can feel all her feels, but we can't talk about it anymore.

It's too hard for me to hear without arguing, or without it becoming personal to me. I have to protect myself and shut that down.

Loving my mom is pretty easy. Feeling compassion for her is very easy. Fighting my own ego is HARD.

A Momversation

Mom: Am I crazy?

Me: No, ma'am. You just have vascular dementia. You are perfectly sane otherwise.

Mom: Can you get me a t-shirt that says, "I'm not crazy, I just have..." what do I have?

Me: VD. I'll get you a shirt that says, "I'm not crazy, I just have VD."

It took her a second, but then my mother laughed like she didn't even have VD at all.

Mom: And that's the truth! Hahahahaha! I have VD and didn't even get to have the fun getting it! Hahahahahaha!

It was a lovely lucid moment of true laughter.

Then she told me someone stood over her bed pouring buckets of water on her head last night, and that the staff were giving people rohypnol and beating them like pinatas for fun. So...

I Want To Get Married

Mom and I were out having dinner and she was acting weird. Weirder than normal. Shifty. She was hemming and hawing around and I finally asked, "Is there something you want to tell me?"

"Well, you know how I told you I've been sitting with Mr. Lloyd at dinner?" It was early days into her Independent Living situation.

"I do," I said.

"He asked me to marry him, but I said I had to ask you first."

I was gobsmacked. You have to understand, my mother married my dad as a virginal 23-year-old. She went straight from her parents' house to his, and never looked back. There was never another man for her. When my dad left her in 1992, she foreswore all men and never even considered dating again.

My mother had been single and angry if you even suggested she mingle for twenty-five years. If she had told me she was pregnant I could not have been more shocked.

"Do you want to marry him?" I asked.

"I do!" She blushed like a tomato.

"Well, then, let's figure it out. I'm assuming he has children?"

And she burbled with delight, telling me all about his kids. They had asked for his kids' blessing first. Mom thought I'd be a harder sell. I was thinking, "If she's got a companion, that's less work for me!"

I was also thinking that it was nice that my mom had decided to love again. She had already turned down the advances of three other gentlemen in her community. I was partial to the guy I had nicknamed Uncle Turtle, but she's got a thing for tall boys with blue eyes, and Mr. Lloyd fit that mostly toothless bill.

Reader, you haven't lived until you have watched an octogenarian tongue kiss your mother through his missing tooth holes, while he gropes her to-the-waist hanging boob. I will never get that image out of my head. Thanks a lot, Mom.

Spoiler Alert: They did not get married. Legalities are complicated when you're wedding in your twenties. When you're closer to death than retirement and you have children who are worried about their inheritance, it's even more complex. Factor in how the government penalizes the aged financially if they marry, and you've got a good case for living in sin.

That was my suggestion when his kids worried aloud about the finances, and Mom and Mr. Lloyd insisted they had to be together or surely die even sooner.

Ultimately, it was a combination of his kids, his former wife's pension, and my recommendation of unholy matriphony that brought things to an end. I was sad for my mom and for myself, seeing all the hours in the day I was planning to get back while she made out with my new dad circle the drain, but I was pretty glad not to have to deal with a group of older stepsisters who didn't seem to like me much anyway.

Before Romeo and Juliet were separated by outside forces, we got pretty far along in talks. I called up a social worker and asked for her advice, then asked around some Facebook groups. If my mother wanted a wedding, she was going to have one. She might not remember she had it, but by god, she would be there in the moment.

Here are some things I learned:

1. If your Loved One is receiving a pension from a

deceased spouse, as soon as they are married to a new spouse, they will lose that income.
2. Your LO's social security payment may change based on the change in marital status and affect their income adversely.
3. Both parties must have the "capacity" to understand they are entering into a contract, and if they show up to the courthouse to get their license and someone is having a bad day and can't remember their boyfriend's first name, the clerk has the right to turn them away.

I didn't worry too much about the money parts. My mom didn't have any, and I figured we'd hire a lawyer to draw up papers saying we didn't want any of his. I did worry a lot about capacity. I wasn't sure Mom and New Dad really understood what they were getting into. I mean, I wouldn't have let my mom sign any kind of contract at that point.

So, I asked her a lot of questions trying to feel out why she wanted to get married, how she anticipated things would change when they were married, and what sacrifices she was going to have to make to share space with this man.

She looked around her apartment and said, "I'm not giving up any of my things. He can get rid of his."

I thought, "These two crazy coots aren't going to make it."

But, I love my mom and she seemed to be really into this dude, and they were already spending their nights together in the love nest of his double bed. The ball was rolling, all I could do was give it the talk and hope it didn't catch chlamydia.

Did you know that older adults are among the fastest growing group for STIs? That is a fact. And just like you would expect a coed dorm at College State University to be rife with herpes, senior communities saw a 23% increase in that very STI in 2019. The olds know how to party.

That means, I had to have the talk with my mother, that my mother never had with me.

When I was sixteen, my best friend came over to my house one day and dumped a purse full of various methods of birth control on my table and said, "I know your parents aren't going to teach you this, so let's go."

She showed me condoms, sponges, spermicides, a diaphragm, and a pack of birth control pills, and gave me a short lecture and demonstration about each, making sure I understood which would keep me baby-free, and which would keep me disease-free, and how to mix-n-match for greater protection.

I was pretty sure my mother had never seen a condom in person.

She accepted my tutelage with good grace and snickers, and I gave her a box of condoms. "Use these," I said seriously. "The last thing you need is syphilitic insanity."

I do not know if she used them. I do not want to know. I do know that when she moved out of that apartment, there were no condoms to be found. Maybe she gifted them to Mr. Lloyd.

After the sex talk (and I had one with Mr. Lloyd, too because better me be uncomfortable and embarrassed than he give my mom crabs and me end up having to treat them), and the money talk, and us meeting each other's families, Mom and Mr. Lloyd started asking me to plan their wedding.

It was May, and Mom wanted to get married in August, after they had moved to their new community together (yes, that was in the works at the same time). Mr. Lloyd wanted to get married in two weeks. "I'm old," he told me. "Move fast."

That was the only guidance I had. Move fast. Mom was all for it. I felt like I was planning a wedding for my pets for all the input they gave me. Honestly, whenever they were together, they were making out. My mom couldn't tear her face away from his long enough to tell me what kind of flowers she wanted.

I hadn't heard back from his kids, so I dragged my feet on planning for them. After all, neither one of them knew how to work a calendar anymore. What did it matter? I sound awful, don't I? I just had a gut feeling this wasn't going to happen, so I was playing it out.

We went to tour the new community and the apartment Mom and Mr. Lloyd would share, when the paranoid side of Mr. Lloyd's dementia flared up. In the apartment, he started accusing my mom of being after his money. My mother returned in kind, telling him he was jealous that she had a better looking child, and that's why he wanted her to get rid of all her pictures of me.

I was 0_o at the sales woman, and she was o_0 right back at me. Mr. Lloyd's daughter was >:[at my mother, so I suggested we break for lunch. We loving daughters took our respective Olds into corners and then away to separate restaurants.

The next day, my mom told me there wasn't going to be a wedding. Mr. Lloyd's daughter had talked him out of it, she said. And she wasn't giving up her pictures of me. That was that.

I say that. Dealing with my mom's heartbreak again was excruciating, and I was glad when Mr. Lloyd moved out into the new community, and Mom started having dinner with Uncle Turtle again. The bottom line is that I will never be able to protect my mom's heart, but at least I protected her bikini area.

I was ill-prepared to protect her from someone else's wife, though. In my mom's first memory care, she met a man she fancied. He had Alzheimer's and didn't remember he had a wife, but his wife was in perfect mental health and did the remembering for him.

At first, my mom was hanging out with him like a boyfriend, snuggling him in the gameroom, and cuddling him in the TV room, but then his wife found out and she started going and sitting up at the community with him all day. If she couldn't be there, one of his daughters was there to make sure my mom didn't lure him off with a siren's call of Wurther's Original and back ointment.

I got a call from the community telling me, "Your mom... I don't know how to tell you this, but she's... She's... She doesn't understand that Mr. Rancher is married and we've tried to separate her from him, but she won't leave him alone. She follows him and his wife around everywhere and won't give them any space." She had even tried to get in the ambulance with him when he'd neededto go to the hospital—she tried to push his wife out so she could ridewith him.

I promised to talk to her. So, just like our uncomfortable talk about STIs, I had to explain to my mom that it's still homewrecking, even if he doesn't think he's ever had a home. She was not pleased with me.

My mom has moved twice since, and she's found a boyfriend in every community. None of them have been as serious as Mr. Lloyd, and I haven't had to watch her kiss anyone, but in her less lucid moments my formerly man-shy mom has been a full on man-eater. "I guess I waited until I was in my 80s to go a'whorin'," she said, getting both her age and her job wrong. No one is paying her. I've done the Death Math. I wish someone would.

A Momversation

Mom: (rambling) ...and I need you to get Robert up here.
 Me: Who?
 Mom: Robert. Your black friend, Robert.
 Me: Er...Mom...
 Mom: (great agitation) You know who he is! Your black friend, Robert! I feel safe with him!
 Me: (struggling to figure this one out)
 Mom: Robert! Robert! Hooberry! Hoo! I mean Hoo! Your black friend, Hoo!
 My dog. She was talking about my dog.

The Paranoia

My mom called me, and I could hear her voice, but it was muffled and far away. After several seconds, I realized she must be holding the phone upside down and backwards. It took another several seconds to be able to shout enough instruction and encouragement to help her turn her phone right side up, and toward her face. Once she did, we had this exchange.

Mom: I couldn't hear you just now because someone got into my room, and got into my phone, and turned it upside down.

Me: Oh. Is that what happened?

Mom: Yes, because when I picked it up it was right side up. But then it was upside down. So someone got into my drawer where I keep it and moved it. And I know that because I went looking for it and it was further back than I had left it.

I think, when you have dementia, it is easier and more pleasant to believe someone is stealing your stuff than it is to accept that you are moving and hiding your own things and a) you can't remember where you put your things, and b) you can't remember moving them in the first place.

I assume my mom lives with that feeling I have when I walk into the living room and forget why I went in there. That's her baseline normal. "What did I come in here for? I know I came in here for something."

I mentioned earlier that I believe my mother suffers from complex PTSD and Paranoid Personality Disorder. Those things don't just go away with dementia. You don't forget you're scared. You just might forget why you are scared, and you lose the ability to reason yourself out of the fear.

Your Emotions

Here's what is going on in my week as I type this: My mom is recovering from what are now four surgeries to remove, repair, and graft over skin cancer on her face. My son and I are both sick, possibly with COVID. Work has exploded and all my clients have gone absolutely insane. And, worst of all, my father is on his literal deathbed in hospice, a thousand miles away. I was able to go visit him just before they started the morphine that would ferry him to the other side in peace, but had to be back home in time to take Mom to what turned out to be that fourth surgical procedure because the skin graft died.

And then my dad died.

I'm tired.

I'm crying at the drop of a hat.

I can't tell my mom about my dad, and it's my mom I want to talk to more than anyone else in the world. But, sometimes she still thinks they are married.

Thirty minutes ago she called me and it went like this:

Ring Ring!

Me: Hello?

Mom: Hi, Laney. What time are you getting here today?
Me: I am not coming over today, Mom.
Mom: Oh. Well, what time are the movers coming?
Me: The movers?
Mom: To take me to that new place?
Me: OH! Oh. Oh... Mom, you already moved.
Mom: I did?
Me: You did.
Mom: But I just finished packing all my clothes.
Me: Um... Well, you moved into your new place a few weeks ago, but you might not remember.
Mom: I'm already here?
Me: Yes.
Mom: So I should unpack?
Me: I think so, yes.
Mom: (starting to cry) This is where I live?
Me: Yes, ma'am. It is.
Mom: (choking on the words) But I have the same problems here I've had everywhere else.
Me: ...
Mom: (crying) I just want to come home. Why won't you let me come home?

Me to Karma: What did I DO?! Seriously, because I'm sure I'm actually and sincerely very sorry for whatever I did to result in this magnitude of...whatever this is.

Karma: Sometimes it's not what you did, Babe. Sometimes, you just suffer the fallout for the choices other people have made. But I know who you are. I know what you're doing. I don't lose an address either good or bad. I got you.

Me to Karma: I don't want other people to suffer my fallout.

Karma: And that's another reason I got you. Remember those back-to-back flights where you had a row to yourself? Keep up the good work, Babe. You can do this.

Me: Mom? I love you. When I come over, how about we go get a banana split? Would you like that?
Mom: Oh! *sniff* I would! *sniff* With extra cherries and nuts?
Me: I'll bring a whole jar of cherries.

Taking Away the Keys

Karma: Atta girl.

"I'm not able to explain what's going on but I need to share my feelings. I'm tired and I need someone to tell me, "I've been there." I need someone to tap on my shoulder and say, "It's going to be okay." I need to hear a "thank you for all that you've done!" I'm tired of this new life. I don't like it. It's so tough. It weighs me down. I'm tired of organizing and managing every single thing. I'm tired of being afraid or thoughtful of what might happen. I'm tired of doing the job several times because she can't remember. I'm tired of seeing them helpless all the time and relying on me." Anonymous

Here's where I want to get really real with you: This caregiving stuff is for the birds. It's hard. It's utterly thankless. It puts you in the awful position of trying to keep someone alive who might want to die, or who might already be dead without your intervention.

That is a special kind of stress because prolonging your Loved One's life prolongs your own agony.

If you are very lucky, you are caring for someone whose presence in your life has only ever added value. You are caring for someone who has always treated you with kindness, love, and respect. You may be facing the horror of experiencing this disease turn a gentle person into a monster, or a robust and active person into a bedbound husk, or a happy, outgoing person into a fright- ened, paranoid goblin.

That personality shift is hard! You find yourself caring for the body of the person you loved after it has been possessed by some alien and unrecognizable spirit. You try to bathe the body, and the hands that used to touch you with love now claw and hit. You try to feed the body, and the lips that spoke such gentle words spit out green beans like a toddler. You try to reason with a mind that usedto be sharp and witty, and now it just sees you as a threat who is hiding all its jewelry.

That's hard work, Friend. That is extremely hard emotionallabor, and that's in the best case.

If you are like me, you are caring for someone whose presence in your life is complicated by a history of abuse. For me, when my mom is having a bad day and is boiled down to the worst parts of her personality and behavior, I recognize the woman who used to abuse me. She's not a stranger. I know exactly who that gremlin is because she used to shake me by the shoulders until I saw stars. She also used to hold me and rock me for hours, while I slept on her shoulder. Our relationship was complex, and that means my caregiving is.

A Momversation

My mom got kicked out of the knitting group in her community because she kept stabbing people with the knitting needles.

I asked her why she was stabbing people with the knitting needles. She shrugged and scrunched up her face like an insolent devil, and she said, "Well, you know they tell me I'm not right in the head, so I guess I just don't know what my hands are doing."

(Keep in mind that my mother also got separated from a group because she kept hitting a man in the head with pool noodles, something I observed. She also kept smacking the same man over and over because she said that way she could keep him awake and interested in life. We've had many discussions about keeping her hands to herself, and about not touching other people with either her hands or objects. I suspect we shall have many more.)

I KNOW some of you are saints, who never see your Loved One as a burden. I know that some of you find great joy in caregiving. You people are jewels in the crown of heaven. I am not that person.

I find no joy in caregiving. I do not enjoy being responsible for the gorgon that inhabits my mother's body. I lost the parts of my mother I enjoyed years ago, and now I am stuck taking care of her body, possessed by someone who rarely even remotely resembles the aspects of the woman I knew and loved.

Now, she is either helpless and needy, or angry and mean. In either case, I have to make choices with every interaction to either treat her the way she treated me as a child, or treat her the way I deserved to be treated. Am I going to let my temper take over and be harsh? Or, am I going to push myself out of the way and be gentle in spite of my own feelings?

A couple of years ago, my mom had just come out of almost three months in the hospital. She was a new resident in memory care, and was learning to put her thoughts, memories, and emotions back together after a stroke and traumatic recovery from an emer- gency surgery.

I was standing behind her wheelchair, brushing her hair for her as gently as I could. She was whining and yowling, swatting at my hands, and telling me I was being rough. Memory rose up in me along with a lump in my throat. I looked at her head and thesmooth, round hairbrush in my hand, remembering the old black- bristled, plastic Goody hairbrush she had used on me, with theridged spine running along the back of it.

My mom liked to backcomb my hair into a puffball for a dressy look. My thin, fine hair wouldn't hold a curl and barrettes just slid out of it, so she was often at war with it while I was sitting under it. When my mom brushed my hair or started styling it, if I yelped, shewould bring the back of that hairbrush down on my skull hard enough to make a cracking sound. I saw stars a couple of times. If I reached up when she pulled too hard, she would bat at my knuckles hard enough to bruise.

I started holding her hair at the root while I tried to work little hospital knots out of the ends, trying my best not to pull at her scalp, and I tried to hold back tears. I was feeling all the helplessness and rage surfacing from my childhood, and all I wanted to do in that moment was hit her in the head as hard as she had ever hit me.

I wanted that. I could taste the temptation. It was bitter, but it promised a sweet reward.

I didn't do it. I couldn't hit her. She was helpless. All she had was her voice and her wayward hands, so I pushed down the rage over how she had taken advantage of my own small head, and I tried to be even more careful with the gnarls at the nape of her neck.

As I was finishing, she said, "Laney... There used to be a little girl. Do you know her? There used to be a little girl, and her mother used to hit her. Her mother would get so angry and she would hurt that little girl."

I took a breath. We were going to do this now? Now, when she couldn't have the actual conversation? "I know her," I said.

"Do you think she knows her mother is sorry?"

"I do," I said, staring at the cowlick in the back of my mom's hair. I had one just like it. No matter what you did, it wouldn't lay right. Even if you got frustrated and hit it with a hairbrush, it wouldn't lay right. "I am sure she knows. And I'm sure she forgave her mother a long time ago."

"I hope so," my mom sighed. "Because she sure is sorry."

People have said to me, "Oh, you're a saint." "You're such a good daughter." "You're an amazing human."

I appreciate that this is what they see. I feel good that nurses, community staff, and waitresses, and my friends see an output that is loving and kind because my insides don't always match. My insides are often angry and outraged.

You know that saying about everyone having two wolves inside them, one bad and one good, and the one that survives will be the one you feed? I live that with every interaction with my mom. That bad wolf? That bad wolf doesn't need a lot of food to stay strong.

So often I am listening to my mother talk and I'm thinking, "You beat the ever-loving shit out of me over something exactly like this. I was nine! I weighed less than fifty pounds!" Or, "You refused to help me do this exact thing, and then you spanked me because I couldn't figure it out." Or, "You shamed me and laughed at me when I did this same thing wrong." And, I want to take that memory and use it to hurt her as much as she has hurt me.

Sometimes, I want to pinch her with words like she used to pinch my skin.

The good wolf tells me, "Lane, your mom messed up a lot.

Hurting her now doesn't change that, and you'd just have to deal with the fallout of her emotional crisis anyway. Be kind. Set your boundaries. Hold the line. Be the caregiver to her you wish she'd been for you."

Sometimes kindness looks like me reaching over and taking her hand, holding it while she talks. Sometimes kindness looks like me redirecting her energy into another conversation.

Sometimes kindness looks like me cutting short a visit and leaving, and taking a couple of days break from her.

Always, I am always aware that regardless of what my mom has done or will do, I have to face myself in the mirror and be a person I am proud of.

That's the wolf I feed.

Because Karma doesn't lose an address.

A Momversation

Ring Ring
  Me: Hi, Mom!
  Mom: Lane! *(rustling sounds, whispering, hand over the phone sounds)* You have got to get me out of here. These people are crazy. They keep moving me from room to room and won't tell me how to get out.
  Me: *(thinking I owe these people vats of well-aged Scotch)* Which rooms are you moving into? Do they have pictures of Thor on the wall?
  Mom: Yes!
  Me: That's your room. Don't you love those pictures? Which one is your favorite?
  Mom: Oh, I know what you're trying to do, Lane Morris, and it's not going to work. You're going to tell me that I'm crazy.
  Me: You're not crazy. I just wonder which picture you like best. I like the one where he is in the tiny tuxedo.
  Mom: That one is fine. But they keep moving me.
  Me: *(I know there are two hallways you can use to get to my mom's room, so when she's confused, she believes she is going into different rooms. Also, she gets lost in the room sometimes, coming out of the bathroom. So she thinks she's gone to a different room.)* Are they taking all your stuff to your new rooms?
  Mom: Yes. But they've stolen my phone. Lane! I need my phone!

Me: Look in your hand.
Mom: Well, I'll be damned. They must have just put it back.
Me: Maybe it was picked up by mistake.
Mom: Maybe. sigh. *Am I crazy?*
Me: No more than you always have been.
Mom: Ha! That's pretty crazy.
Me: It's an acceptable amount.
Mom: (laughing) So, how is your day?

I Can't Do This Anymore

There will come a breaking point for you. When you have a Loved One with dementia, you are facing stressors mentally, physically, and emotionally. It may be the toll of having to keep up with the doctor's appointments. It may be the toll of having to lift their walker or wheelchair into the back of your car. It may be the toll of listening to them beg to go home. Something is going to tip the balance and you're going to feel like it's all going to come crashing in on you.

You need two things: You need support groups and time off.

Support Groups

Support Groups are pretty easy to find. I belong to several on Facebook. In the middle of the night, sitting beside my mom's hospital bed, worried I was going to get fired from my job for another unexpected absence, and crying because I was so tired, being able to log on and share with, and be supported by people who had been in the same position was a lifesaver.

Just knowing you are not alone in your experience, that you are not alone in what you are thinking or feeling can be a huge benefit.

I have learned new methodologies and found resources like

Teepa Snow in my groups, and I have loved being able to share information when I've seen something new.

For example, I ran into an on-site urgent care provider in an elevator one day. She told me that they did same-day urgent care visits to private homes as well as senior communities, and that they accepted Medicare. She gave me a folder full of information.

I took pictures of the info and posted it in a group. Soon, other members from all over the country were responding with similar information. We created a little resource network for people who needed help, who might not be able to travel for care.

Time Off

I don't think I can say enough times, you do not owe your LovedOne your life. Whether this is a parent, or a partner, or even your child, you do not owe your Loved One every breath in your lungs and every ounce of strength in your body. You are allowed to have time to yourself. You are allowed to take care of yourself.

No amount of work or love is going to turn back the clock, or change what dementia has done to your Loved One. If you could love someone out of dementia, there wouldn't be an Alzheimer's association.

If you aren't healthy, you can't help anyone. That goes for your physical health as well as your mental health.

I was sitting with a friend who was telling me about her father's struggle as the main caregiver for her mother. She said that he had been talking about suicide as a way out, but she wasn't sure if she should take him seriously. I told her she should. Suicide rates among caregivers are high. When you don't see a way out of the darkness, when you are looking at the rest of your life and all you can see is the struggle of caregiving, death can seem appealing. It can be easier to wish for your own death than to face the shame and guiltof wishing your Loved One would die.

I want to be sure you know it's okay to have those feelings–to wish your Loved One would die. That's a normal feeling and you don't need to be ashamed of it. Just don't act on it and murder your Loved One. That's bad. That's a crime.

Anyone who has ever been a caregiver knows that you're not

really wishing your LO was dead. You're wishing your LO was healthy so you wouldn't have the burden of their care. Health not being an option, death is the only relief available. I want you to know that I understand that. If no one else ever says this to you, I am saying it to you right now: I get it. And it's okay to have those feelings.

It's okay to be tired. It's okay to need a break. It's okay if you don't find joy in cleaning poop out of your dad's butt crack. It's okay if you hate clipping your mother's toenails. It's okay if you are grossed out by your spouse's drool. If you are showing up to ensure their safety and health, whether that be as a visitor to their community, or in your own home, you are doing the job. You don't have to love the job.

Caregiver should not become your identity.

I watched my mother break herself on the wheel of caregiving. Her worth became inextricably entwined with my grandparents' health. As they diminished, so did her self-worth. With every setback, my mom lost a little more of herself.

You cannot beat dementia. You can provide comfort and care for your LO, but you cannot make them whole again. Their lack of wholeness might mean they don't even recognize that you are providing comfort and care. They might think they are abandoned and abused, regardless of how much time and effort you are putting into them. You will never be able to do enough to restore their minds, and that might mean letting go of hope that you can hold onto their hearts.

It's sad when a parent no longer remembers a child, but I've witnessed a special kind of grief in women whose husbands have forgotten they were married to them, who have turned their charms onto my mother. I have had to watch a woman sit on one side of her husband while he held hands with my mom on the other side. My heart broke for her.

Little by little, she decreased her visits, from being with him from the moment he woke up until the staff put him to bed, to visiting until noon, to visiting every other day. It was sad, but at the same time, I had so much respect for that woman. She was able to separate the love she had for him from who he had become, and she was able to live a life outside of his disease.

    I realize this is yet another thing on your to-do list, but you must find time for yourself, and you must engage yourself in a hobby, or a job, or a social circle outside of caregiving, or you will look up one day and realize that caregiver is no longer something you do, it is who you are. Dementia wants more than just your Loved One. It wants you, too. Punch it in the face.

A Momversation

I had my mom on speaker phone, not realizing Thor was lying on the floor behind the couch. I thought he was down the hall in his room. When we hung up, I heard this little "mip" noise.

"That's so..." His voice broke. "Sad."

I try really hard to shield him from the sad bits, and only let him into the funny, or sometimes the angry bits because those are easier to explain and deal with. I can explain being enraged by my own futility or even resentful of my mom's earlier life choices much more easily than I can explain the depth of her despair and hopelessness.

I agreed with him. He wanted to know how we could help. All we can do is answer her phone calls and listen, and try to encourage. All I can do. I'm not putting him on the phone because she's not lucid and I can't trust her not to say to him what she says to me.

Consenting Adults

Can we talk about a touchy subject?

Literally?

Recently, I saw a discussion in a support group, and a caregiving woman was asking for advice about what to do when her dementia-suffering spouse rejected her physical affection. I've been in a caregiving position for grandparents and parents, but never a spouse. I cannot even imagine how much it must hurt when your spouse rejects you because they can't remember who you are, or your rela- tionship to them.

However, I have been the recipient of unwanted physical attention from a Loved One who was confused about my relationship to him, and I know exactly how upsetting and frightening that can be.

Friends, if your Loved One rejects your physical affection, stop touching them. Don't try to force your LO to accept your kisses, your hugs, your pats, or your heavy petting. If your LO is confused about who you are and you are forcing yourself onto them, that's not right. That's rapey. Don't rape your Loved One.

I've seen other discussions where caregivers are upset because they no longer want to respond to their LO's advances because the relationship dynamic has changed so much that having sex with the person who used to be their favorite partner is just a disgusting thought. That's okay. When you're changing someone's diapers and having to remind them who you are fifty times a day, it's okay to not want to have sex with that person, no matter what your love life was like even two years ago.

When you become someone's caregiver, the relationshipchanges, and it's okay if your desire wanes. I write that and I think about the women who are caregivers for husbands whose personali- ties have completely changed with dementia, whose once gentle spouses might now be forcing them into sex, or who have become physically violent. Please ask for help. Regardless of your Loved One's diagnosis, you deserve your own bodily autonomy and you donot have to be anyone's punching bag.

If you are a husband caring for a wife who has become violent or aggressive, please ask for help. You deserve to be safe and not have to live with threats, or attacks.

Please don't abuse the person you are caring for, and please don't let the person you are caring for abuse you. If you are afraid you are going to hurt your LO, or if you are being hurt by your LO, there is a national hotline you can call at 800.799.SAFE (7233). In either situation, they will help you.

And listen, you may get to a point of frustration where you want to lash out at your Loved One. Caregiving is a terrible job. Having the feeling is normal and it's okay to have the feeling. Do not act on the feeling. Do not hurt your Loved One. They can't help who they have become any more than you can help who you have become in response to their changing needs. Get help for yourself so you are able to help them.

While we're on consent, I've seen several people in support groups ask how to deal with giving their Loved Ones access to grandchildren. Every situation is unique, but I stand by this: Kids shouldn't be forced or shamed into spending time with or touching people that make them feel uncomfortable. I know how hard it is for me to process everything going on with my mom, and I'm a full-grown adult with fifty years of coping mechanisms in place. There is no way I am going to ask my child to battle the same demons.

Does seeing my son make my mom happy? Indeed! Does she remember she's seen him? Nope.

My mom and my son were BFFs until she went into memory care. His middle school was across the street from her independent living community, and he walked over to see her every afternoon because he just enjoyed being with her. But then she started getting really weird with him, and was often confused about whether he waswith her, or not.

The night she had her stroke my mother called everyone in her phone book (except for me) and told them that my son had been with her in her room, but she had gone to the bathroom and he had been kidnapped and she needed help finding him. She was so convincing, workers from her senior community were out walking the neighborhood looking for him because she said he had been taken from her apartment.

He had not. He was with his dad and me at the movies. He had been with her earlier in the day as we had toured new communities. He'd had lunch with her, and he had helped carry some of her groceries back up to her apartment, and he had talked with her while I refilled her medicine bags. She had hugged him goodbye and told him to enjoy the movie as we left.

That night kicked off three months of hospital/nursing home/psych ward stays, her concerns that I was a prostitute, that sharks were swimming around in her bedroom, and that my son was engaged to a cafeteria lady and had three kids of his own. It culminated in a dramatic shift in her personality and ultimately, memory care. My son doesn't need to be around who my mom is now, unless he's feeling it.

I have seen people say, "You need to make your kids visit because they'll regret not having spent time with their grandmother when she dies." I call bullshit on that. You might have complicated feelings around denying Grandma access to the children she loves so much, but what you're really doing is protecting your children from distress, and giving them autonomy, helping them understand that their consent in spending time with people is important.

Don't force your kids to walk this path. If they want to tag along with you, as my son regularly does, bring them along, but don't force them.

Time Off

You have to have a break. You must take a break. You are not an island and you cannot do this alone.

If you do not have anyone to watch your LO, check in with your state's Department of Health and Human Resources. You likely have access to respite care funds that would allow you to bring in a qualified sitter to give you a chance to rest. (I realize I may be saying that to someone who has a full-time job, who can't sit on hold for the amount of time it takes to connect with a government agency, much less take the time off to file paperwork. Here, I point you to FMLA. Even then, if you're waiting tables, or a nail tech, or a daycare worker, you might not be in a position to use FMLA. I don'thave any answers, and for that I am deeply sorry.)

When Mom and I were caring for my grandparents, my uncle would come down twice a year and stay for a week. For a few days of each of those two weeks, my mom and I would go stay in a hotel and just sleep. Well, I slept. I deal with stress by hibernating. My mom would just sit quietly and stare at the ceiling.

Now, my mom is in memory care. I live nearby, so I go and visit her twice a week, and I take her out for adventures a few times a month. Once a month, I take a weekend off from visiting.

I had a really hard time doing that at first, but she doesn't remember when I've visited anyway, so she's not hurting for my company. More to the point, I work a full-time job, have a family to care for, and life to live. I need time off for myself. I deserve to have a weekend where all I have to worry about is the grocery store, the laundry, and squeezing in as much time with my teen as he'llgive me.

And, sometimes, if my mom is being really combative, or she's behaving in ways that make it difficult for me emotionally, I will take time off from a visit. I deserve to be mentally and emotionally healthy. I deserve to set boundaries to protect my heart. So, I do.

You are allowed to take care of yourself, so take time off.

Something I've Learned

I write a lot about and I talk a lot about how I suffered generational abuse. My grandmother was abused, so she abused my mom. My mom was abused, so she abused me. It's really easy to read about that and think, "What monsters!" My grandmother was actually a monster, but she was my monster and I loved her fiercely.

I didn't realize I was being abused as a child. The bad things that happened were all just folded in with the good things. The same hands that hit me, held me. The same voices that screamed at me, sang my praises. It wasn't all bad, or all good. It was just my life. One of the many therapists I worked with said, "A goldfish doesn't know when its bowl is dirty. That's just its bowl."

It wasn't until I grew up and moved away, and started trying to form adult relationships that I realized I had some major emotional health issues. In working to fix myself, I saw where I had been broken in the first place. It took me years to be able to say that my mom abused me. I felt like I was betraying her to even suggest she was less than perfect. I struggled to match the appropriate emotions to memories, dissociating from my right to feel angry or hurt by how my mom's mental health, co-dependency and insecure attachment style affected me.

It took me another long while to realize that I have the capacity to love my mother for all she did right, hold her accountable for all she did wrong, and forgive both the things she remembers and forgets. As a parent, I recognize that my mom made active choices to hurt me when other options were available to her. As a parent, I also recognize that making those choices requires a commitment to being your best self. I have mental health care available to me that my mom did not.

I am hyper-honest with myself about my feelings now. When I am angry, or resentful, or hurt, or sad about my mom's situation, I name the feeling and I let myself feel it. I work through it. I try to understand the root of it. If it's something I can change, I move to change it. If it isn't something I can change, then I just let myself have the emotion. Feeling resentful isn't bad. Acting out against my defenseless mother because I feel resentful is bad. I've learned the difference between having the feeling, and doing the feeling.

I am regularly resentful that my free time is impacted by my mother's poor choices. That's okay. I still take my mom to the doctor because it would be wrong to let her suffer just because I'd like to have that extra hour of sleep. I did not choose to have this responsibility, nevertheless, it is my responsibility and I will accept that (and all the feelings that go with it) and do a good job of it.

And that's a good place to be to hop into the next section and talk about what the world around you thinks of the job you're doing.

Your Extended Family's Emotions

Wheelchair Quarterbacks

Right off the bat I want to tell you this: If your family isn't actively helping you, you don't need to listen to anything they say. In fact, they can go talk a long walk off a short pier. If your family isn't in the trenches with you, working to support you as you care for your shared Loved One, they have no right to offer any criticism.

If you are caring for a shared Loved One, your family should be hands-on, elbows deep in the adult diapers with you on a regular basis. One week every six months doesn't count. Phone calls and greeting cards don't count. If your family isn't losing the same amount of sleep you are sitting up with your Loved One, using the same amount of vacation days you are ferrying your Loved One to necessary visits, breaking their backs in the same way you are to physically support your Loved One, they can just zip their lips and crawl back into their hidey-holes.

Right here, right now, I give you full permission to ignore, block, delete, unfriend, and slam the door on anyone who isn't helping you, who is saying you aren't doing enough.

Over the course of adopted uncles, grandparents, and my mother's illnesses, I have come to hate the words, "You are a saint!"

I'm not a saint. I'm not even a martyr. I'm a regular human being who is doing normal life things. Are the normal life things fun? No, they are not. Do they make me exceptional for doing them? No, they do not. If there were any way I could get out of doing them with a clean conscience, would I get out of doing them? Yes! Absolutely!

And that is how a lot of Caregivers who have siblings end up doing all the work alone: because their siblings can get out of the work with a clear conscience by deferring all the load to one brother or sister.

"I just don't have the same kind of time Jane does."

"I couldn't keep Mother at my house because it would ruin my marriage."

"Bert is single, so he is better for Dad to live with."

"Martha lives two hours closer, so it's easier for her to be involved."

"Doug has more money, so it's okay for him to take a bigger chunk of the cost of memory care."

I'm an only child, so I don't have to fight with anyone to help me. I'm just on my own anyway. I have a full-time job, a family, a social life, a mortgage, upcoming college costs, my own retirement to plan, and every aspect of my mother's life to consider. I've made it work because I don't have any way out of making it work, short of letting her keep her car keys and possibly kill herself and other people while she's out joyriding.

We do what we have to do. I feel lucky that I don't have the additional drag of family members who won't help, or whose help is a pittance, or who criticize me regularly for what I've tried to do.

Nosy Neighbors

You know who does criticize me? I'm laughing as I type this. The lady at the front desk of my mom's community. She thinks some of my visits are too short, and she tells me about it. I got a survey from the community recently and that was the only negative thing I had to say about them.

That lady doesn't know anything about me, other than how many minutes I spend in my mom's room. She doesn't know how or why it is so hard for me to even show up sometimes, or why some of my visits are under an hour. I always shoot for an hour, but my mom gets bored with me these days and she'll say, "Well, I shouldn't keep you," which is Southern for, "Get out." So, I get out.

Prior to my mom's big decline, she had begun to alienate everyone who showed an interest in her. She burned bridges with family and friends. When she moved into independent living, there was only one person left in her life who would come visit her, and she destroyed that within months. When she had a stroke and I needed help with her while she was hospitalized, no one would come. I finally found one of her old friends who would come visit if I paid her. I had to pay one of my mom's old friends to visit her.

Now and then, I'll get a text message from someone who used to work with my mom, or one of those people who was a friend in her before-times, and they will shake a finger at me for talking so openly about my childhood and how my mother chose to parent me. They feel like I'm being unfair to her. She can't defend herself.

Part of me agrees with them. My mom can't defend herself, and I struggle with whether or not that is fair. You know who else couldn't defend herself? Four-year-old me when her mother was raising welts on her legs and back with a switch. Ten-year-old me when her mother was pinching bruises into her arms as entertain- ment, then threatening her for crying. Fifteen-year-old me who was expected to just stand still and let her mother slap blood into her mouth.

What defense is there for that? She didn't know better? Someone had done it to her? That's just how things were done? No. Otherwise, my son would have been little more than a greasy spoton the wall by now. Otherwise, I'd have used the same hands on herthat she used on me.

Am I a coward for only talking about it now that my mom can't jump in and say why she did those things, or apologize publicly? Possibly. Very much possibly. Here's another truth: I was still really afraid of my mom up until I needed to be her caregiver.

In the past, whenever I tried to talk to my mom about how I felt, she would become irrationally angry and/or hysterical. She would accuse me of being a traitor. She would tell me how she'd poured her whole life into me, and only ever loved me, and demand toknow what she had done wrong that I had turned out this way. She would insinuate that my words were making her suicidal. Her favorite line to use was, "You treat me worse than a dog." It's still her favorite line. She uses that every time she asks to come live withme and I say no. And, she still threatens suicide if I won't give her what she wants.

I tell the truth because I have to face it in order to be what my mother needs. I tell the truth because someone else out there is experiencing the same thing I am, and maybe no one's ever told her that she's worth saving, and she needs help. I need to tell the truth because it is the truth and because when we hide abuse, we allow it to continue.

When we hide child abuse we make space for elder abuse. We can't be squeamish about holding people accountable for their behavior, otherwise, that bad behavior breeds.

I tell the truth to hold myself accountable. Sometimes, because my mother hit me, I want to hit her. Sometimes, because my mother said terrible things to me, I want to say terrible things to her. Sometimes, because my mother unburdened herself onto me with problems beyond my ability, I want to burden her. I say those things out loud to face my demons and hers.

Because I know what my mom did was wrong, I choose to try to do what is right. And sometimes that means instead of spending an afternoon with her, I do a fifteen minute visit to make sure she has pull-ups, clean sheets, clean hair, clipped toenails, a full belly, and a kiss on the cheek. I'm okay with that. I'm the only person who has to be okay with that.

I don't know your situation. I hope you are caregiving out of a loving, peaceful place. I really do. If you aren't, please know you aren't alone. And please know that as long as you are not abusing your Loved One (physically, verbally, emotionally) and you're doing your best to keep them safe, you don't need to listen to what anyone thinks you should do differently.

A Momversation

My mom has been on a manic-calling streak, meaning she dials me at least once every hour, sometimes multiple times an hour (five dials between 9-10AM today). I answer once every three hours (so that she doesn't panic and think I've been kidnapped, or am "throwing her away" and make life harder for her caretakers.)

Every call starts with her asking what I am doing. I tell her I am working. She asks, "Still?!" I answer, "Always." She giggles, then sometimes tells me what she wants, and sometimes pouts that she knows she's bothering me, wanting me to tell her she is not a bother—which I do because she can't remember how many times she has called me, or what we talked about when.

This most recent call was her demanding candy.

And it's calls like that, after I hang up, I think, "I am truly a decent human being." Because I am patient and kind with her, even when I want to drive down to the memory care, take the phone, and snap it in half and just scream bloody murder until dementia is so afraid of me, it flees her body.

The Long Haul

When you spend as many hours in the car as a child as I did, especially on road trips, you develop a time-callous. There is a helpless inevitability to a road trip when you are a forced passenger. You have no control over where the car is going, where it will stop, when it will start again, or even the station playing on the radio. You are utterly at the mercy of the driver.

From 1981 through 1999, my mother and I drove the distance between Dallas, Texas and Fort Benning, Georgia at least four times a year, sometimes more. It was 743 miles between our front doors. We usually made it in about twelve hours, stopping about every three in Welcome Station rest areas. Most of the time, we did our driving through the night, and most of the time, nothing was open outside of public rest stops. By the time we would hit Selma, Alabama, the Hardee's would be turning on its lights. So, I always looked forward to stopping there, but between Shreveport and Selma, we drove on wishes and prayers.

I remember us praying to make it to that one gas station in Union Town, AL most trips. I remember that trip when Mom was afraid the car wouldn't start if she turned it off, so she left it running while she filled the tank, that trip where we had to pull over every

The Long Haul

few hours and let the radiator cool down, the trip she got three speeding tickets in a row, and the trip after my father left, when she played Garth Brooks's song, "The Dance", on repeat from Dallas to Montgomery.

That last one... Friends, I begged and cried for her to turn off that song as she sobbed along to it. Halfway through Mississippi, I lost my cool and screamed, covering my ears and stamping my feet against the floorboard. That only gave me reprieve for as long as it took me to finish screaming, and for her to wail that I didn't understand. No, I didn't. I still don't.

I'm not sure how to express the frustration and helplessness I used to feel in the passenger seat of my mom's car, or how often I had to face down my own temper and subvert my own needs and desires so she could drive to Georgia without me causing trouble, but it formed who I am. I'm not sure it formed me in a healthy way, but those hours of being forced to practice self-control molded me into who I am today. It formed how I face adversity. It formed how I work through my mom's illness. I just keep going. I don't know anyother way than to just keep going.

In 2006, there was an ice storm in Dallas. I got caught in a traffic jam on an overpass, where cars were at an absolute standstill. After an hour, a woman got out of a car a few vehicles ahead of me, and started running and screaming, her arms flailing in the air. She ran around and around, screaming until she slipped and fell. I watched two men get out of neighboring cars to help her back into hers and I had this epiphany: That woman looked exactly the way I had always felt halfway through road trips with my mother, especially that Garth Brooks trip.

I had a crazy woman on the inside of me, screaming and flail- ing, but I had learned to put her on mute in order to avoid getting popped in the mouth, screamed at, or backhanded into the sidewindow. By the time I was a teen, I knew how to grit my teeth and just get through Birmingham. I would dissociate from my feelings and force my mind into a daydream. I recognize these are notexactly healthy traits, but they have served me well as my mother's caregiver.

The Long Haul

Dementia has both my mom and me trapped in a car on a terrible road trip. Neither one of us can get out of this car. We're just in it. Period. Some roads are going to be smoother than others, but all of them are going to be long, and we're not stopping until this is over. Eventually, we'll make it to our destination, but only one of us will be getting out of the car alive.

I wish I could leave you with an uplifting story, or a glimmer of hope. I can't. If you are caring for a Loved One with dementia, it's going to suck, and it's going to suck until they die, and then it will suck in a different way. I'm such a ray of sunshine.

The hope I can give you is this: If you take care of yourself, face your own demons, give your Loved One care with gentle hands, and do your best, you're going to be okay. And you being okay will make things better for someone else.

Like Garth says–no. I still can't do it.

But you can.

You've got this.

Help Lists

Following are some checklists, websites, and phone numbers that might be helpful to you in your journey.

Important Paperwork Checklist

- Power of Attorney
- Medical Power of Attorney
- HIPAA Release Form
- Medical Advance Directive
- Living Will
- Last Will and Testament

Personal Identification Checklist

- Social Security Card
- Driver's License
- State ID Card
- Birth Certificate
- Passport
- Insurance

- Medicaid

Important Information Checklist

- Banking information
- Bank Name
- Checking Account Numbers
- Savings Account Numbers
- Investment Account Numbers
- Safe Deposit Box Numbers & Keys
- Online Banking Information
- Credit Cards
- Car/Boat/Other Vehicle Titles
- Deed to House or Land
- Lease agreements
- Insurance Policy Information
- Life
- Health
- Auto/House/Other

Bills to Look For Checklist

- Mortgage/Rent
- Auto/Other Vehicle
- Insurance
- Life
- Health
- Cable/WiFi
- Property Tax
- Water
- Electric
- Other Utilities
- Credit Cards
- Taxes

Medical Information to Know Checklist

A Workbook

- Primary Care Physician
- Specialists
- Cardiologist
- Oncologist
- Psychiatrist
- Neurologist
- Ob/Gyn or Urologist
- List of Medications (including dosage and when it is taken, example Metformin, 500mg, 2x daily at breakfast and dinner)
- List of health conditions
- List of surgeries and/or hospital stays
- Family history of illness
- Allergies
- Height
- Weight

Websites/Apps to Make Your Life Easier

(Listed are sites I have used personally and with which I have had good experiences.)

- Eldercaredirectory.org/federal.htm to help you find Federal Government Programs for Seniors
- Eldercaredirectory.org/state-resources.htm to help you find state and local assistance for Seniors
- Care.com to help you find sitters, drivers, nursing
- Aplaceformom.com to help you find senior living communities
- Caring.com to help you find senior living communities
- Instacart.com to help you get groceries, snacks, and personal items to your Loved One on an as-needed basis
- Amazon.com to help you set up subscription service for items your Loved One needs replenished on a regular basis
- UberEats, DoorDash, and GrubHub to help you deliver hot meals to your Loved One

- Cookiedelivery.com or Tiff's Treats to help you say thank you to the people providing care at your Loved One's community, or to the dentist who takes extra time and care of your terrified Loved One, or to the friend who helped get your Loved One to the dentist when you couldn't get the time off work, or just to yourself because you truly deserve a cookie, Friend. If you don't have a Tiff's near you, I'm sorry!
- Zocdoc.com to help you find doctors, review doctors, and set appointments
- YouTube.com to help you find videos (like Teepa Snow's) about dealing with dementia
- Theconversationproject.org to help you have a conversation with your Loved One about their wishes for care

Important National Phone Numbers/Hotlines

- Social Security, Medicare Part B, and Supplemental Security Income: 1-800-772-1213 toll-free. If you are hearing impaired and use a TTY device, call 1-800-325-0778.
- 211 is a national resource number that covers all 50 states and serves as an information and referral number. You can call and ask about caregiving or aging related resources in a particular area.
- Elder Abuse Hotline (National Domestic Abuse Hotline) 1-800-799-SAFE (7233) toll-free. If you are hearing impaired and use a TTY device, call 1-800-787-3224.
- Eldercare Locator, a public service of the U.S. Administration on Aging connecting you to services for older adults and their families: 1-800-677-1116.

A Workbook

Questions to Ask on Community Tours

- Are your prices all-inclusive, or are there additional fees based on levels of care?
- What is your level of care pricing structure?
- If my Loved One needs more care in the future, what does that look like in your community?
- How do you plan for elopement?
- What is your procedure flow if my Loved One has a fall, or a sickness?
- Do you have easily accessible toilets in common spaces?
- How often is laundry done?
- What happens if my Loved One has a toilet accident?
- What kinds of activities do you have?
- How do you get residents to engage in those activities?
- What happens when a resident is having a bad day, and might be acting out?
- How do you respond when a resident thinks they have experienced a theft?
- What religious services do you have available?
- What toiletries do you provide?
- Do you accept automatic shipment deliveries?
- If you see a resident is running out of important personal items, what do you do?
- What happens if a resident is aggressive or violent?
- What happens if my Loved One is hurt by another aggressive resident?
- What transportation services do you provide?
- Do you take residents to doctor's appointments?
- Do you work with any visiting physicians?
- Do you work with a particular pharmacy? How are prescriptions managed?
- If my Loved One wants to call me, how can they do so?
- Can you tell me more about the negative reviews I've seen about your community? How do you address the concerns raised in those reviews?

- What happens if my Loved One passes away in your care?
- How many meals are included in my Loved One's rent? Are snacks included?
- What happens if my Loved One is still hungry after a meal?
- Can my Loved One have snacks in their room?

Things you Need to Remember to do for Yourself

- Schedule and keep your own annual physical, and follow up on any lab work results–how is your Vitamin D?
- Take time off from continual care for your Loved One– remembering that care is not just physical. If you've spent a lot of time on taxes, or scheduling appointments, or visiting, remember to rest your brain.
- Do something you enjoy.
- Go stand outside for a few minutes and just breathe.
- Ask for help.

Notes

The Stages of Dementia: Alzheimer's and General Dementia

1. *Types of dementia*. (n.d.). Web MD. Retrieved October 22, 2021, from https://www.webmd.com/alzheimers/types-dementia

Caregiving for Someone Who Abused You

1. Cleveland Clinic. 2021. *Paranoid Personality Disorder: Symptoms, Diagnosis & Treatment*. [online] Available at: <https://my.clevelandclinic.org/health/diseases/9784-paranoid-personality-disorder> [Accessed 8 December 2021].

Acknowledgments

I would like to thank my husband and son, who have poured so much of themselves into me so that I had resources to pour into my mother. I thank my friend group for being the support and sounding board I have needed, especially the worst fake sister in the world, Lori-Anne Cohen, the best chosen-sister in the world, Jamie Anne Grimes, The Alphas (Irene Ferris, Darice Moore, Lisa MudanoDalton, Deborah Pettingill, and Holly Bird), Angela Lopez, and Renae Redwine Perry. Thank you to Joshua Lee, whose intervention on my mom's behalf through her banking habits helped me understand how serious her issues were. Thank you to Chastin Miles and Anne Barron, whose professional services have added years to my life. Thank you to TJ Jones, who has been a mini-mom to me since 1986, and to Don and Tommie Buckman who have been more than in-laws, loving me like I'm their own since 2004. I am extremely grateful for the support and advice I found in the Purple Sherpa Basecamp (Dementia Family Caregiver Support Group) on Facebook. You all are the reason Loved Ones are capitalized throughout this book. I am also grateful for Sara Lunsford, whose editing elevated an okay book into a good book. Most of all, I thank my mother, Joan Morris, for doing the best she could with everything she had.

About the Author

Lane Morris Buckman is a writer and illustrator, masquerading as a techie by day. Her writing oeuvre is as random as her professional resume and includes the cozy mystery, Tiara Trouble, the early-reader, picture book, My Rainbow World, and the smutty romance, Playing All the Angles, under the pen name, Nicole Lane. A quick Google search will bring up vampire novels, more cozy mystery, and non-fiction contributions about parenting. Lane was a cast member of the 2015 production of Listen to Your Mother Austin, where she shared the story, My Son Hits Like a Girl, a love letter to her own mother about all the things she did right as a parent.

www.ingramcontent.com/pod-product-compliance
Lightning Source LLC
Chambersburg PA
CBHW070539010526
44118CB00012B/1179